Praise for *The Wisd*

"In **The Wisdom of Sam**, Dan
reminds us of the simplicity of the things that matter, their
abundance in our daily lives, and the power of love to reveal
us as whole. Dan is the grandfather each of us would wish
to have and Sam, the grandchild who is life's greatest gift.
A book that is food for the journey."

— **Rachel Naomi Remen, M.D.**, author of
My Grandfather's Blessings and *Kitchen Table Wisdom*

"Another beautiful volume from one of the few inspirational
writers who has actually walked the walk and not just
talked the talk. Gottlieb is a national treasure."

— **Daniel Gilbert**, professor of psychology, Harvard
University; author of *Stumbling on Happiness*

"**The Wisdom of Sam** offers a compelling journey with
a compassionate and insightful guide, Dr. Dan Gottlieb. I was
sad when the book ended—loving this course in how to open
our eyes and hearts to the fullest—and profoundly grateful for
the vision this book so magnificently provides to appreciate the
wondrous gift of being alive. This is an irresistible invitation to
seize the moment and awaken our minds to live life fully present."

— **Daniel J. Siegel, M.D.**, best-selling author of *Mindsight*

"This is a heartwarming book written by the grandfather of
a young child with an Autism Spectrum Disorder. The
relationship between the two is remarkable, in terms of
understanding each other's point of view and life experiences.
The book can be read at many levels, from a description of
autism in a child and quadriplegia in a mature adult, to a
philosophical understanding of the meaning of life. I really
enjoyed reading the words of wisdom in **The Wisdom of Sam**."

— **Tony Attwood**, author of *The Complete
Guide to Asperger's Syndrome*

The
Wisdom
of
Sam

Also by Daniel Gottlieb, Ph.D.

LETTERS TO SAM: A Grandfather's Lessons
on Love, Loss, and the Gifts of Life

LEARNING FROM THE HEART: Lessons
on Living, Loving, and Listening

VOICES IN THE FAMILY: A Therapist Talks
About Listening, Openness & Healing

VOICES OF CONFLICT; VOICES OF HEALING:
A Collection of Articles by a Much-Loved
Philadelphia Inquirer Columnist

The
Wisdom
of
Sam

OBSERVATIONS ON
LIFE FROM AN
UNCOMMON CHILD

DANIEL GOTTLIEB, PH.D.

HAY HOUSE, INC.
Carlsbad, California • New York City
London • Sydney • Johannesburg
Vancouver • Hong Kong • New Delhi

Published and distributed in the United States by: Hay House, Inc.:
www.hayhouse.com • *Published and distributed in Australia by:*
Hay House Australia Pty. Ltd.: www.hayhouse.com.au • *Published
and distributed in the United Kingdom by:* Hay House UK, Ltd.: www
.hayhouse.co.uk • *Published and distributed in the Republic of South
Africa by:* Hay House SA (Pty), Ltd.: www.hayhouse.co.za • *Distributed
in Canada by:* Raincoast: www.raincoast.com • *Published in India by:*
Hay House Publishers India: www.hayhouse.co.in

Design: Jami Goddess

Library of Congress Cataloging-in-Publication Data

Gottlieb, Daniel
      The wisdom of Sam : observations on life from an uncommon
child / Daniel Gottlieb.
            p. cm.
      ISBN 978-1-4019-2385-3 (hbk. : alk. paper) 1. Conduct of life. 2.
Autistic children--Family relationships. 3. Grandparent and child. 4.
Gottlieb, Daniel, 1946- I. Title.
      BJ1521.G6355 2010
      305.9'085--dc22
                                                    2009034949

Hardcover ISBN: 978-1-4019-2385-3
Tradepaper ISBN: 978-1-4019-2388-4
Digital ISBN: 978-1-4019-2798-1

14 13 12 11   5 4 3 2
1st edition, April 2010
2nd edition, April 2011

Printed in the United States of America

To Sam and all the Sams in this world.
Who are able to see things we can no longer see.
Who know things about the joys of life,
the beauty of nature,
and the opportunities each moment brings—
those things most of us have long since forgotten.
May they be patient teachers
and we their humble students.
So that we may rediscover what
we have always known.

CONTENTS

INTRODUCTION

When my grandson, Sam, comes for a visit, we usually have breakfast together. The conversation is pretty much what you'd expect between an 8-year-old and a 62-year-old. Our morning talks often focus on juice and cereal. We might discuss going to the arcade later in the day. Or, if Sam is in the mood, he will tell me about his friends in school or how he feels he is doing in wrestling this year. And, inevitably, we will pay a lot of attention to our dear friend Loki with the soulful eyes and light auburn hair. As Loki is a dog, his mood is mainly dependent on one factor—whether he has been fed or not.

During the morning's transactions, Sam will give me a big kiss. And before breakfast is over, we will usually find something that amuses me and sends Sam into gales of laughter.

In other words, it's a normal morning. Sam is bursting with energy and eager to get a start on the day, but each of us has our limitations. I'm quadriplegic and will spend the day in my electric wheelchair. And Sam is a child with autism. It is hard to tell that Sam is different. That is, until he runs into children his own age, or is asked to leave his mother, or faces an unforeseen turn of events in the day's schedule.

These limitations don't matter. We are who we are.

I started writing letters to Sam when he was born. A lot has happened with Sam, with his parents—my daughter

Debbie and her husband, Pat—and with me. When I first noticed symptoms of autism, and Debbie and Pat got a diagnosis, we had no idea what would happen to Sam as he got older. Would he be able to talk, attend school, and get along with other children? The word itself, autism, covers a wide range of possible symptoms and outcomes— what is referred to as a "spectrum." The diagnosis does not give any prediction about where a child will be on the spectrum. So there was no way for us to anticipate future challenges. But having an early diagnosis, in itself, proved extraordinarily important, and soon Debbie and Pat were using all the resources they could find to help Sam make his way in the world.

Letters to Sam, completed when Sam was five, expressed the hopes, fears, and unconditional love of a grandfather finding his way with his grandson. Both discovering, each step of the way, the possibilities of that relationship. However, the correspondence was all one way, from Pop (as he calls me) to Sam.

Now Sam is growing up. Our relationship has gone through many transformations, but perhaps the best of all is the way he has become my teacher.

❖❖

Shortly after I started writing this book, I happened to have dinner with my friend Linda Welsh, a psychologist who works with medical residents at the University of Pennsylvania. Linda is affiliated with a program in which each resident is assigned to a family that is dealing with a severe chronic illness. After meeting with the family, the resident visits the family's home throughout the year, learning what it's like to live with chronic illness.

While doing follow-up with one of these families, Linda spoke with an 11-year-old boy who had severe rheumatoid arthritis. Linda asked the boy how he felt about the resident who had come to visit him. "He was really cool," the boy replied. Then Linda asked the 11-year-old what he liked best about being with the resident. The boy thought for a long time before he replied: "I got to be the teacher, and it feels good." No surprise there. Any time someone is genuinely interested in our lives, we feel dignified and respected. But when it is an adult allowing the child to be the teacher, that is a gift that can have a lasting impact.

All of our children have something of critical importance to teach us, but are we able to be their students? I believe we do have that capacity, if we respect their wisdom.

In *Letters to Sam*, I told the story of how each of us got an indentation on the upper lip before we were born. As the story goes, God whispered all the secrets that we need to know in order to live our lives. Then he, or she, said "Sssshhhhhhh" and pressed a finger to our upper lip.

Those are the secrets that Sam and all of us were born with. We know them, but that knowledge can be easily lost. In many respects, children are more honest than adults, because they are not yet influenced by expectations of teachers, peers, and the larger world. So what they say is their truth, and what they see is more clear than what we see.

As Sam's grandfather, I see him as a child who is different from other children. His character is uniquely his own. Sam is loving and engaging. He has eyes as big as the moon that seem to be asking questions even when his lips don't move. When Sam does say what he thinks, he speaks without editing himself, often expressing thoughts that are surprisingly kind and considerate and often remarkably insightful. He remembers rules and is quick to remind me of them—especially when I'm not following them! The Sam I know, and love, often can't differentiate between appropriate and not-appropriate timing for these reminders, but if his confusion makes him stumble a bit socially, to me that's all the more endearing.

But for all his uniqueness, Sam has many traits in common with children who see the world differently than many of us. Now that Sam is talking to me about the world, there are numerous times when I'm aware he actually sees it more clearly than his parents or I do. How can this be explained? Often these children are not influenced by context. The positive side of this is that they can see things we miss—the texture of a paper with an important message, the exact words someone used at a critical moment, or the colors of the sunset when everyone else is rushing around. But this clear and narrow focus is also one of the reasons their social skills are often so poor. They cannot absorb all of the social cues in the environment. For example, Sam would be comfortable going up to a group of peers and trying to engage them. But he wouldn't be aware that they were already having a conversation, so he would just begin saying whatever he wanted to say. And then he wouldn't be able to notice that the kids might be uninterested. Sam's focus would be exclusively on the story.

Sam has improved dramatically since his initial diagnosis, but he still has that clear-minded perception. And because Sam is doing so well, he is able to talk about his inner experience.

But . . . is he really wise? Can a seven- or eight-year-old teach us anything truly important?

These were some of the questions that led to the writing of this book. If I have accomplished my mission, this book is not only an introduction to Sam's world seen through Sam's eyes; it is also a reminder of the things we once knew and might otherwise have forever forgotten.

꿎꿎

Implicit in this book, as in *Letters to Sam,* is another question that, I hope, will fascinate you as much as it does me. It is something that many of us ask about our children and grandchildren. Who is this person? And what will he or she be like as an adult?

Author and physician Rachel Naomi Remen tells a story about a gift from her grandfather. It was a clear plastic glass that contained a seed. When she wanted to know what kind of seed it was, her grandfather merely said, "Make sure it's watered and has plenty of sun, and you'll find out."

Rachel dutifully did as her grandfather requested, and eventually she saw a little sprout. She called him on the telephone and again asked what it was. Same answer. Every time she called, she asked the same question, and each time his answer was the same.

Our children are a lot like that seed. We cannot know what they will be. And we certainly cannot make them into the children or adults we want, but we can love and nurture them nonetheless. Sam changes almost every day. He started off as a delightful, smiling, and fully aware baby. And then his parents and I watched him change. The light seemed to go out. That's when Debbie and Pat had him tested and learned that Sam had a pervasive developmental disorder, which placed him on the autism spectrum. He didn't speak, and he banged his head on the floor when he got frustrated.

And then, after two years, with the help of various therapies and his own development, he began to speak— at first with a speech impediment and then without. We watch him now, and he is thoroughly engaged, delightfully empathic, and loving.

On a recent visit, Sam asked my nurse to put me on the sofa so he could lie on my lap while we watched a movie. And then in the middle of the movie, we just looked in each other's eyes for a while and said nothing—in that silence, feeling great love for one another.

He's had plenty of water and sunshine. He will continue to unfold and blossom, I hope for the rest of his life.

∽ॐॐ∾

For my own part, I can't say Sam's birth has made me different, but it has brought a new kind of love into my life—a kind of pure adoration that doesn't come with a sense of responsibility other than to love this child fully. His birth has also given me the great gift of watching my own child become a loving and devoted mother.

Sam's birth has also made me feel more comfortable with growing older. When I look at Sam, I know that I will not see much of his world, that my life is finite, and that these moments are precious.

I have always been a loving man, but the role of "grandfather" has given me more freedom to love. Whatever might have been inhibiting my deep, affectionate caring for the people in my life ended with Sam's birth.

So now I am a man with more faith in the innate health of living beings. As a result, I sit with my patients and there is a loving twinkle in my eye. I know that they will be okay. We just don't know what that "okay" will look like.

My lectures always conclude with the importance of love, telling people to love who they love and how to do so better. Because of Sam and everything he represents, my deepest wish—my daily wish—is to make the world better for my Sam and all of the other Sams by making it more loving and compassionate. I want to do this through my writing and lectures, through my relationships with friends and family, and through my interactions with people I encounter in daily life. The book you now hold is an expression of that wish.

CHAPTER 1

Just a Little Forgiveness

When Sam was younger, he loved to draw pictures with crayons. As a budding artist, he was a study in concentration. There was something princely about the way he sat at the kitchen table, his feet dangling, his thick brown hair bowed over the sheet of paper that commanded his complete attention. When he concentrated really hard, his tongue poked out of the left corner of his mouth.

I don't know where his artistic inspiration comes from, but I do know that it has been encouraged by his mother, Debbie. We all learned shortly after his diagnosis that loving adults in his environment needed to keep him engaged so that he wouldn't get lost inside his mind. Debbie has been with him constantly and involved with his activities from then on. And with that safe and secure presence, Sam began to flourish; over time, we all watched him become more engaged and more comfortable in his world. So whenever Sam sat down to draw pictures, Debbie stayed nearby, her presence providing reassurance. And when Sam became wrapped up in what he was doing, it was clear that he was not getting lost inside his mind anymore. Still, he relied on Debbie's presence, and sometimes he would call on her.

When Sam makes a picture, he is keenly aware of color, and nuance is important to him. This is not unusual for children on the autism spectrum: they are very sensitive to sensory stimulation and the wrong color can be visually irritating. I became aware of this when Sam was about six years old. He and I were talking and I happened to make some comment about a green shirt someone was wearing. "Actually, Pop, that's aquamarine," Sam said matter-of-factly, not knowing that his pop really had no idea what aquamarine was.

Though that was the first time I learned about Sam's acute awareness of colors, Debbie found out much earlier. One day when Sam was about five years old, he sat down to color a picture. Debbie, as usual, was nearby, and Sam asked her to hand him crayons as he named the colors. Though Debbie was doing her best to assist Sam, she was also trying to finish up a number of things in the kitchen, which left her momentarily distracted. She wasn't paying close attention when Sam requested the color turquoise. Debbie glanced quickly at the crayons in the box, picked one, and handed it to Sam. Unfortunately, the crayon she handed him was light blue.

On the verge of applying crayon to paper, Sam's hand froze in midair. He seemed shocked. Raising his dark eyes to regard his mother, he spoke with an uncharacteristic edge in his voice.

"Mommy, I asked for turquoise."

Debbie retrieved the light blue crayon and handed him the turquoise one.

Sam's searching gaze never left her face. He studied his mother, trying to fathom what had gone so terribly wrong.

"Mommy," he concluded. "You weren't paying attention!"

"I know, Sam," Debbie confessed. "Will you forgive me?"
Sam thought for a moment.
"Just a little," he said.

৵৵৵

I'm not sure that I, or Debbie, or anyone but Sam would
have felt what he was feeling at the moment he realized
the awful truth—that his mother (such a seemingly caring
and loving human being!) had betrayed him in so casual
a manner. To most children with autism or Asperger's, a
milder pervasive developmental disorder, the devil is in the
details, and Sam is no different. When things are orderly
and predictable, his comfort increases, but surprises are
deeply unsettling. Now that Sam is eight, while surprises still
come thick and fast, he can often identify what's bothering
him. When he was younger, that wasn't the case, and he
responded in ways that disturbed and frightened us. There
were tantrums that reached a level of uncontrolled violence
when, for no obvious reason, he would repeatedly bang
his forehead against the wall or floor. Sam didn't speak
until he was nearly four years old, which only added to
his frustration with the world. But by the age of five—with
steady therapy and guidance from family and teachers—Sam
had come to a much better understanding of what distressed
him, and he was starting to learn how to tell us. There were
no more head-bangings and fewer tantrums. Obviously,
Sam felt great frustration at finding the wrong color crayon
in his hand, but he had been able to explain the source of
his frustration!

So I admired the way Sam expressed himself. I also
admired his honesty about forgiveness. Sam, to his credit,
understood how much he could forgive. His mother asked for
complete and categorical forgiveness. Sam couldn't go that
far. What he could manage was to forgive her "just a little."

❦

Hearing Sam's words, I felt as I often do—that his starkly honest and unmediated response conveyed his own particular brand of wisdom. Sam, like all of our children, has something to teach us. This time, the lesson was about honesty and forgiveness.

Some time later, as I was preparing a talk on the topic of forgiveness for a group at Villanova University, that incident with Sam came back to me. I also recalled a letter I had received from a young man in South Korea. Unlike Sam, my Korean correspondent had been deeply influenced by religious education. He accepted the tenets of his Christian faith while grappling with his own conflicted feelings, and that had brought him to an impasse. Though he struggled at times with the English language, the essence of what he wrote was this:

> Sometimes I feel that it is not easy for me to forgive someone who has inflicted severe pain on my heart. I know that I have committed many mistakes with my neighbors, brothers, and sisters . . . therefore, I know that I have often received forgiveness from them and I will have to beg forgiveness from them in the future. However, because I am not a perfect person, sometimes it is very hard to forgive my colleagues who have hurt my feelings—which eventually causes depression. I know that Jesus asked us to forgive our brothers and sisters, always and consistently. However, I am not a perfect person like Him. *Sometimes, what Jesus asked of us sounds like another violence to me.* Because I am not a perfect person like him, it is very difficult for me to live like him.

Violence! Imagine that.

What's violent about what he believed Jesus asked of him? Perhaps at the deepest levels, it feels violent when we ask things of ourselves that are unreasonable. Here we are, after experiencing an injury, being told that the right response is forgiveness!

What if, instead of placing unreasonable expectations on ourselves, we take a look at who we are and what has happened to us? Once we get away from the lofty theological, philosophical, and psychological preaching, this whole business about forgiveness is really just about managing injury. It's about finding a way to live with injustices, large and small.

❧☙

When we are dealt an injustice, it comes as a shock to the system. A number of times, I have been asked to describe the car accident that left me a quadriplegic. What I learned, some time after the accident, was that an entire wheel and tire had broken loose from an oncoming truck, flown across the road, and landed on the top of my car. My only memory of that moment—and the answer I give—is simply this: "I was hit by a black thing."

After that, life as I knew it was forever changed. But I also believe it is an accurate metaphor for what happens to all of us when we experience trauma. A black thing comes out of nowhere, and in an instant life is altered. Isn't this what happens when we experience a divorce or the death of a loved one? In an instant, we are in the grip of a disaster that destroys the world as we know it. One moment, we are walking down the sidewalk on a sunny day, and the next moment there is no sidewalk. No sun. And no day. Only darkness.

Afterward comes confusion and terror. But somewhere in the mix, most of us experience a silent rage because we feel something has been *done* to us or *taken* from us against our will. As we carry that rage, we look for a target and yearn for justice. I spent over a year with seething rage that was directed toward the truck driver, having violent and sadistic fantasies. Then I found out that a tire and rubber company was the cause of my accident, and I wished a lifetime of unhappiness for those who contributed to my suffering. The truth is, for most of us, justice represents just one thing—the ability to reclaim what we have lost. It is the longing for what we had yesterday or the day before.

And, of course, when we try to pursue justice that way, we fail. Every time.

∽❧∾

I'm sure each of us can describe the essence of an injustice we've experienced. For me the injustice originated in the engineering department of a prosperous, cost-conscious tire-and-rubber company where massive metal wheels for trucks were being designed. A number of people in that company knew their wheels had a design flaw. Under certain circumstances, a truck wheel could come loose from one of the trucks that they put into production. The wheel could fly across the road or down the highway and land on top of a car. And if that happened, the passengers of that car could be killed or injured. Knowing all of this, they made the decision to go ahead and build an unsafe product. That is how, and why, I was injured.

For Sam, the fact of the injustice is a turquoise crayon instead of a blue one.

The stories differ, but the experience of injustice is similar for all of us. When we *experience* it, we feel shock, outrage, and helplessness. And we realize how extraordinarily vulnerable we are.

So how do we cope with these feelings? Clearly, what has happened to us is *wrong*. If the injury was perpetrated by someone, then that *person* is wrong. I knew the company was wrong and I was an innocent victim. Knowing that, we open the gates to great anger and righteous indignation. We mobilize those around us to agree about right and wrong, to assure us how entitled we are to our anger. So we wrap these feelings around us like a threadbare coat in a snowstorm in an effort to protect ourselves from our own vulnerability. It doesn't help, but it's all we have.

❧

My dictionary defines *forgiveness* as a "letting go of resentment." I'm sure that's what forgiveness is supposed to be. But how do we let go if we believe our anger protects us from further injury or, in some strange way, holds a perpetrator accountable? Resentment and righteous indignation distance us from our own pain, and we need distance to survive. At least initially. But when resentment continues, it becomes toxic.

It might not matter whether *they* are wrong where we are right. What matters is that we were hurt and forced to suffer. What matters is that we lost a piece of our life, and now we are vulnerable. What matters is that we need compassion, and the safety and courage to feel what we feel. When that happens, when our suffering finds its voice, our heart softens and opens. And rage turns to grief—a deep and heartfelt grief for what we have lost. In the ideal world, the person who hurt us would bear witness to our pain and feel genuine remorse. But that is often impossible. What is possible is for us to bear witness to our own lives. To listen to the suffering with compassion, sadness, and love. And then it is safe to grieve.

So, how does grief turn into forgiveness?

I believe forgiveness is a spiritual process, which requires faith. Not necessarily faith in a higher power, but faith that broken hearts heal. Faith that we have all of the resources to recover and be loving and compassionate once again. Faith in the knowledge that true healing is not about reclaiming yesterday but fully opening up to today.

∽⁊❧∾

When I wrote to my Korean correspondent, I told him Sam's story. And then I added:

"Sure, Jesus talked about forgiveness, but he also talked about caring for those who suffer. The reason you have closed your heart to those who hurt you is because you suffer. And the longer your heart stays closed, the longer you suffer. There is only one thing that opens hearts: compassion. Do you think you could offer yourself compassion? When you are hurting, do you think you could love your wounded heart without hating someone else at the same time?"

After I mailed my letter, I realized that there was something else I wanted to add. I wanted to say: "Don't worry about forgiveness. Allow your wounds to heal. Allow your heart to heal. And then use the wisdom you have acquired to help heal the world. Don't pursue forgiveness. Allow it to follow in the wake of your life. True forgiveness asks you to be able to find the other person's humanity. You cannot do that until you find your own."

∽⁊❧∾

When we are wounded and alone, we need people who love us enough to look in our eyes and see our suffering. That's what Debbie did for Sam. She was able to see that he was truly hurt, not by the turquoise crayon but by his mother's distraction at a time when he needed her full attention.

If Sam had behaved in a more "grown-up" manner, perhaps he would have felt obliged to try to forgive his mother completely. Perhaps he could have reflexively said, "Yes, I forgive you, Mommy," without even noticing that he was hurt. Or he could do what most adults do: forgive out of fear of causing conflict. Or he could hold a grudge so that he could have the illusion of control.

But there is too much tenderness in Sam. He was hurt, and he knew it. Perhaps, in some way, he also knew that this small injury would heal. So he forgave his mother as much as he could—"just a little."

And then, as always, life went on. Sam never did any more work on his forgiveness. As far as Debbie could tell, he thought no more about it. Whatever sense of injustice lingered inside him probably dissipated quickly. That's what happens with children. They somehow know that hurt feelings get better.

Maybe that's another lesson we need to learn from them.

CHAPTER 2

Permission for Happiness

I've noticed that a lot of us haven't figured out where happiness comes from. For most of our lives, we are taught that happiness is a destination. We are trained to believe that achievement and accomplishment will bring happiness. We convince ourselves that material goods will bring us a level of security that will lead to happiness. We tell ourselves that if we do whatever we can to avoid what we fear, we will be okay. Then and only then will we be happy.

The road to happiness can, ironically, feel long and torturous. Making matters worse, the road rarely gets us to our ultimate goal. But whenever I hang out with kids I am reminded that we adults are missing a lot of shortcuts.

I am writing these words a few days after a visit by my friend Amy and her five-month-old son, Jake. Some construction work was being done on Amy's house, so she asked if she could come over for the day. I said sure, but let her know that I was working on this book and I wouldn't have much time to be social. Shortly after Amy and Jake arrived, I went to my office and got down to work.

They were in a secluded part of the house, but from my office I could hear distant sounds. Usually I just consider it background noise, and I don't pay any attention. But after a little while, I realized that the sound I was hearing was Jake giggling. I stopped working to listen more carefully.

There it was again.

I tried to concentrate—after all, I had work to do! There I was, trying to write about compassion and being awake to your life, and that distracting noise kept drawing my attention away from what I thought was the "real" work! There was a part of me that was frustrated and anxious, as I had a self-imposed deadline. But something inside that was deeper and more alive drew me to that sound like a magnet.

What was it about Jake's giggle that was so attractive?

Well, we know about the biochemistry of laughter and how it releases endorphins in the brain that make us feel better. We also know that laughter cuts down on stress, but there's more. Laughter gives us a taste of what everyone wants—happiness. It's just that simple.

A while ago, I was seeing a woman in my office who seemed to be carrying the weight of the world on her shoulders. Her daughter was away at college and calling every day. She was in a marriage that was deteriorating, and she was angry—at her husband, at her mother for not being more supportive, and at just about everybody else.

Finally, after ranting mindlessly for a few minutes, she realized what she was doing and said, "Do you think I'm nuts?"

I hesitated for a minute before I made eye contact and said, "Yes, I think you're nuts. But just a tiny little bit!"

And we both laughed. Nothing changed in her life, but in that moment of laughter, she was happy and secure.

◈

Intellectually, I know that when people become adults and begin listening to their demanding egos, they start taking themselves too seriously. Way too seriously. I mean waaaaaaaaay too seriously. Things that feel important to adults really are funny when you think about it. Silly, in fact. Drop in on most adults' minds, almost any time, and you will find those minds somewhere in the future, planning for things that will probably never happen. And then we worry about those things, and then we worry about how we will be seen or how our children will be seen.

We worry about stuff that most kids find silly. As a matter of fact, one of the reasons we love kids is because they have yet to master the fine art of worrying. Kids know that most of this worrying stuff is silly. We forget. And then we start teaching them that our way of thinking is right and theirs is wrong. Sam is tuned in to this secret. From the beginning, it seems, he and I have both been trying to teach each other about being silly. But I think I've learned a lot more from him than he's learned from me. I need more help letting go than he does. And Sam is a great teacher when it comes to letting go. In his mother's view, the two of us are pretty impossible together. We get *the look* a lot. Probably deserve it. But once you let go, it's hard to stop.

∽ᇮᇔ

Almost from birth, Sam has been an expert giggler, and he loves it when we all join in. Before he could talk, he realized there was quite a lot he could do to make us laugh—from joyous hugs to funny facial expressions. But most wonderful of all was to hear *him* erupt into gales of laughter.

Shortly after he learned to talk, his mom and I were amused to see him trying out something that I used to do myself when I was a kid. Sam had been watching television sitcoms, trying to figure out what it was in those shows that made people laugh. He figured that if he memorized the sentence that came just before the laugh and repeated it, people would laugh at *him!* Even now, at the age of eight, he will memorize a joke and repeat it to make the people around him happy. Not that he always understands why people are laughing. But sometimes, he realizes, it's worthwhile to try anything to make people laugh.

Sam knows—though not consciously, of course—that when other people around you are laughing, it doesn't necessarily mean they like you more (although they might). It goes beyond that. When people are convulsing with laughter, even for a moment, you feel connected, joyful, secure. Just for that moment, everything is just right. So Sam likes to make people laugh. And so do I.

Sam's funniest joke right now goes like this:

Question: "What's invisible and smells like peanuts?"

Answer: "Bird farts."

That's funny? Listen to him tell it, and you'll crack up. Why? Because he cracks up. That's the only reason.

My father was the same way. He was the easiest man alive to tickle, both physically and metaphorically. When we would go into the Army-Navy store he ran, I would pick up a pair of socks and tickle the bottoms of the socks, and my dad would laugh like crazy. When he got older, I would tell him my favorite dirty joke about senior citizens in a nursing home, and he would giggle the same way he did 50 years earlier. That was one of my great joys—hearing him laugh.

❧❧

Not surprisingly, since Sam and I are both guys, our forte is bathroom humor. When Sam was four and just beginning to talk, he and I would go out for a walk together around the neighborhood, taking note of all the stuff that was going on. I told him to watch out for camel poop.

"Why camel poop?" he asked. He was on to the joke right away but went along with it, which gave me great joy.

"Well, Sam, if you find camel poop, there's bound to be a camel nearby."

So he started looking. Fortunately for Sam, there are plenty of dog owners in the neighborhood who don't pick up after their pets. Pretty soon he was asking, "What about that?"

"That? No, that's bear poop."

"Well, what about *that?*"

"Could be lion poop. Definitely not camel poop."

Finally we identified a deposit that *might* be camel poop.

"You think?" he asked, going along with the game.

"Only one way to tell. If it's really soft like a Tootsie Roll, it might be camel poop. You have to pick it up."

"I'm not going to do that," he said, giggling.

"Then how are we going to know if there's a camel around?"

So it went. We did find some poop that looked like camel poop. Sam, to his credit, stuck to his hygiene. And we never saw a camel. But hope springs eternal.

Of course, now that he's older, a few more subtleties are possible. Sam knows, for instance, that I really don't like being bald. So he torments me about it. I try to be a grown-up, knowing this joking is all in good fun. But I'm *really* not happy about being bald. I tell people that if there were a cure for baldness and a cure for spinal-cord injury, I'd be in the baldness line first. (After all, they've developed really good wheelchairs for people with paralysis, but there's no decent solution for baldness.) So my rebellious little grandson sees how to get to me. He especially likes to ride on the back of my wheelchair and say, "Keep going, my trusty steed!" while he pats me on my head. So I'm trying to be a grown-up here, and I'm starting to fail at my efforts. So now I have to get him back. And good.

"Sam," I say, "this is genetic. Do you know what that means?"

He shakes his head. This gives me the opportunity to explain that baldness is an inherited trait. It comes from his grandfather on his mother's side. I'm his grandfather on his mother's side. So if I'm bald . . .

"This," I say, patting my head, "is your future."

"No!" he hollers while giggling at the same time. "No, *you're wrong!*"

But he knows I'm right.

"This is you, Sam. This is you."

And we laugh.

∼⋑⋐∽

One would think that an old coot (as Sam frequently calls me) would be disappointed that I can't teach a young lad any great lessons about happiness. I would perhaps be a more conventional teacher if I could tell him, in all honesty, that he could achieve happiness by working hard, obeying rules, being kind and generous, or following all 12 points of the Boy Scout Law. In truth, some of those guidelines might contribute to his happiness, but I don't know. I have to be honest in admitting that they might not. Sam understands that happiness is about being near people we love, giving and receiving kindness, and giggling several times a day.

Every day. No matter what.

Wouldn't it be wonderful if Sam could teach that simple lesson to the whole world?

And sometimes that giggle is the only lesson we need.

CHAPTER 3

We're All Together

Spooky was a big black dog, a mix of Labrador and German shepherd, with pointy ears, a flat head, and a long nose. He was spirited, happy, and very friendly, and had the kind of tail that could knock you over if you got in the way of its wagging.

When Sam came along, Spooky was getting on in dog years, but they took to each other beautifully. Sam would throw his arms around Spooky's neck and hug him recklessly while the dog just stood there, eyes widened in blissful enjoyment. When Spooky lay down for a nap, Sam would nestle alongside him.

Of course, living in a bustling household with an energetic young boy and a semi-tolerable cat named Bullwinkle, Spooky was also subjected to a fair amount of torment in his retirement years. For example, Sam had a handheld laser light. He discovered that if he made the beam of light dance around, Bullwinkle would chase after it. Sam also learned that if the laser light played over the hind end of the sleeping Spooky, Bullwinkle would pounce on the septuagenarian's hindquarters. Spooky would jump up in alarm, wakened from his slumber by the impact of cat's claws on his resting behind.

If Spooky resented the hard treatment, he never let on. Perhaps somewhere in his dog brain, he wondered why his backside held such an attraction for Bullwinkle. But he didn't blame Sam. On Sam's part, there was delight in knowing that he could control an interspecies rivalry with nothing more than a beam of light. But clearly he adored Spooky.

Spooky had been part of Debbie and Pat's life for many years before Sam came along, and as adults, they knew that a big dog was not likely to live more than 15 years. Sam was just 7 and Spooky was 18 when Debbie and Pat found out he had cancer that was destroying the bone in one leg. Soon he would be unable to walk. His life was coming to an end.

Debbie and Pat decided to tell Sam on a Friday night. They explained that Spooky would die soon, so they needed to get all of their loving in quickly. Sam cried and cried. He cried until he almost threw up. And then he stopped. The next day, he didn't want to talk about it anymore. When the vet came by a couple of days later to put Spooky to sleep, Sam seemed removed from what was going on. He played with Bullwinkle. He asked a few questions. But basically he had done all his grieving.

Not so his parents. Both were in great pain. Debbie had been attached to Spooky for many years, and her grief was deep. Pat cried, too. Looking at his grieving parents and Bullwinkle, Sam grew thoughtful. He seemed to be working things out. And finally he announced his conclusion.

"The important thing," said Sam, "is that we're all together."

❧❧

Sam's comment was partially an observation and also, in part, a wish that everyone stay close during these painful times. He was giving voice to a universal human longing that is expressed around all the rituals, but mostly around grief. That longing is to be in a nurturing community.

The Jewish ritual of shiva reflects that beautifully. When my sister, Sharon, died, shiva was held at her house. It was the first time I had experienced such an outpouring of support from a community. Food appeared. Then people appeared to serve the food and clean up. People came to talk to us about Sharon and their experiences with her. We all felt held together by her community.

I experienced this again when my father died. That was years later, and since I was the last immediate family member, shiva was held at my house. This time it was my synagogue community and my personal friends who swept in and supported me. And I felt cared for and loved. It felt safe to be in a community focused on my welfare. This was the first time in my life that I had no responsibilities, which allowed me to just mourn. I could feel my pain while surrounded by people who loved me. Yet, at the same time, I felt extraordinarily alone because I was literally an orphan.

Such is the human experience. The longing to be together, to be fully understood, to be loved and taken care of when we need it most—such is the heart's longing in all of us. But at the same time we can never be understood because of our uniqueness, because the deepest parts of our beings cannot be described in words. What I've learned over the last 30 years is how that uniqueness, which can make us feel so alone, also shapes our personalities and gives each of us the freedom to become who we are. At the same time, we live with the feeling of being alone in the world.

᪐᪐

All transitions are difficult, and the transition from life to death is the most difficult of all. All change involves loss, and all loss must be acknowledged. In one of her seminars, Rachel Naomi Remen said, "Fear is the friction in all transitions." We resist most transitions because, as a species, we find security in sameness. If we believe that tomorrow will be pretty much the same as today, we are more secure in the predictability of our lives. This is true even if our day-to-day lives are unhappy. This might be another of life's great cosmic jokes—that predictable sameness makes us more secure and yet the only thing predictable in life is change.

A world without Spooky. That's what Sam had to face. And on the Friday night when he couldn't stop crying, I'm sure that's all he saw—a world in which he could not wrap his arms around his dog, or curl up next to him while he slept, or tease him with the aid of a laser light. Before that day, if Sam desperately needed something, it would be provided. But now, for the first time, Sam needed something that the people who loved him couldn't provide. Sam realized that his longing for more time with his precious dog would not be met.

The next day, and the day after that, and the day when Spooky was put to sleep, Sam noted that his parents were still there and so was Bullwinkle, and he began to see the world he and his parents would inhabit as they survived this transition. Not without grief. Not without pain. But together.

When I had my accident, I was terrified of the transition from a "normal" life to the world of disability. All I wanted was what I had yesterday, when I hadn't known how precious that "normal" life was. And that's really the nature of all pain and all transition. We want what we had before. But most of us make our transitions one way or the other.

I was at Jefferson Hospital for about ten weeks of acute care until my health was stable. After that, I was moved to

Magee Rehabilitation Hospital, where I would remain as long as the doctors and therapists felt I was making progress. At Magee I had a highly structured schedule of occupational therapy in the morning, physical therapy every afternoon, with meals in between. For six months I followed the same pattern every day.

When it was time for me to leave, I went around the hospital saying goodbye to all the people I knew. Having been there for so many months, I had grown close to the staff. We had shared many stories about our lives. These were the people who cared for me, taught me how to live my new life, and accepted me for who I had become, which engendered deep friendships. Nevertheless, when it came time for discharge I was supposed to be happy to be leaving and going back to my real family. In fact, I was terrified. All I wanted to do was stay in the hospital where it was structured and safe and my needs were cared for. When I got home, I just wanted to go to bed and stay there. After suffering terribly with my transition from normal to disabled, I suffered again with this new transition. I didn't know it, but I wanted a community of people who could relate to my suffering. And I didn't have one. There were plenty of people who loved me and who cared for me, but nobody really understood.

I felt so alone in the middle of a family I adored. My secret wish was to go back to the hospital, but I was far too ashamed and guilt-ridden to tell anyone that. So I felt even more isolated.

For years I felt that sense of aloneness was my cross to bear, and it triggered all sorts of emotions, from shame and insecurity to anxiety and resentment, ultimately leading to depression. And then something happened. Instead of fighting with my aloneness, instead of considering it a problem to be fixed or a burden to live with, I simply let go. And when I did, I began to view this thing called aloneness through curious eyes.

As I grew more comfortable with this simple fact of my life, I began opening up to others about it. I talked about it with my psychotherapy patients and on my radio show. I wrote about it in my books and articles, and in the process I made an interesting discovery. The more I opened to aloneness, the less alone I felt. The reality of the aloneness has never changed, but the more comfortable I have grown with it, the more I feel part of a larger community that shares these feelings.

If Sam had been older, I would have told him that death is the most painful of all transitions and that the deeper we love, the more we suffer. I would have told him that when we lose what we love, we inevitably feel alone, because love is a personal and private emotion. Sam's relationship with Spooky was his own. The feelings he had when he lost Spooky could not be fully understood by anyone else, including his parents, even though they loved Spooky, too. But maybe Sam didn't need to hear that last part. Because he spoke the words as a child that I learned as an adult: "At least we are all in this together."

And what a blessing that we are.

CHAPTER 4

I'm Sumfing Else!

When Sam was about four, every now and then he'd present Debbie with a little comment or accomplishment that would amaze her. And whenever he did, Debbie would say, "Sam, you're something else!"

"Yup," he would reply. "I'm sumfing else all right!"

As Sam got older, the challenges got bigger. We wondered if that wonderful self-assurance would always be part of his nature. Debbie wanted to reinforce his self-confidence whenever possible, so that if all went well, Sam could hold on to that terrific feeling that he sure was sumfing else.

But we knew it wouldn't always be so easy for him to feel that way. It isn't for anyone.

One day in early June when Sam was eight years old, his father, Pat, suggested that the whole family spend the weekend at their beach house in Ocean City, Maryland. Pat had to play in a golf tournament on Saturday, but he figured Sam would have a great day at the beach. There was a further incentive. A friend of Pat's (known to Sam as "Mr.

Pete") would also be spending the weekend, bringing along his kids, Howard and Billy, who were about Sam's age.

For Sam, the beach house is a big playground. The living room of the house is set up like a game room, with foosball, a pinball machine, and an electric golf game. Across the street is a clubhouse with a pool room and a Ping-Pong table. In the evening, the kids and parents head to the boardwalk with its multitude of attractions.

Debbie realized that it was impossible for her to get away for the weekend because she had a mountain of work to do. But if Pat went ahead, played in his tournament, and Sam went down to the shore with Mr. Pete, Howard, and Billy, they would all be together Saturday night. Then Sam could make the return trip with his dad. There was just one flaw to this plan. Sam would have to be away from his mother for a whole night, and he hadn't done that before.

Was it possible for Sam to make this trip without her?

For another eight-year-old child, a night away from his mother might have been no big deal. And besides, his father would be staying with him. Isn't Dad as good as Mom when it comes to providing security?

Not quite. Most children with autism spectrum disorders experience substantial anxiety. The source of this anxiety is partly organic: the areas of the brain involved with autism are also involved with creating anxiety. But partly the anxiety is reactive. The world looks very different to an autistic child, whose perceptions and sensations can make things feel pretty scary. Therefore, these children often feel right on the verge of losing control. Experts say the classic "autistic meltdown" is what happens when a child's sensory system goes from being on the cusp to being overwhelmed.

So what do we do when we feel anxious? The research shows that we tend to clutch what is familiar. But we don't really need research to tell us that. When religious people feel out of control, they pray more and attend services more.

When alcoholics feel out of control, they drink more. Same with workaholics. Often, following a sudden loss or trauma, people rigidly cling to their routines. Whenever we feel anxious, we hold on to what we know. For Sam, the most secure thing in the world is his mommy.

Debbie provides safety. Like many parents of disabled children, she anticipates the problems her child may have and tries to prevent those problems from happening. Debbie's protectiveness comes from her altruistic love for her child and from her own anxiety, but it's the protectiveness any of us would feel if our child were more vulnerable than others. I've watched Debbie work for Sam's rights in many ways—as an activist for justice, as a healer, as a nurturer, and, perhaps most of all, as a warrior. This is the good side of anxiety, and this is why Sam feels so safe with his mother. What if she's not there when he begins to feel overwhelmed and anxious, in an environment that seems to be out of control? His dad's presence is not quite the same. He adores his father and loves to play with him. But safety? That's Mommy's turf.

Debbie and Pat knew that Sam's night away from home would be a great adventure, but it could also activate his anxiety. Throughout his entire young life, Sam had never traveled without his mom. Whenever they visit a strange house—even mine—Debbie is with him. Each stage of the trip is carefully outlined for him: "We'll be in the car for three hours, and you may be uncomfortable at times, but if you are, you can tell me about it. We'll stop at that place where you like to walk around and get some ice cream. And as soon as we get to Pop's house, you can put on your roller shoes and ride behind his wheelchair. You'll sleep where you always sleep at Pop's house."

All this preparation, Debbie has learned, is essential for an autistic child. In fact, Debbie has taken advantage of an extraordinary computer program called Boardmaker, a

Mayer-Johnson product that actually helps parents outline each day—working with their child to explain the plan, answer questions, and describe each event that is likely to occur. When they're planning a trip, Debbie uses the Boardmaker to help Sam visualize what's going to happen in the beginning, middle, and end. They also discuss what could happen to interfere with their plans or change the routines, but these possible changes are bookended by predictable events.

If Sam went by himself, he would be forced to face unfamiliar situations that could feel chaotic and disturbing. Sam knew the beach house, so it wasn't exactly foreign territory. But there were other things—many things—that could be terribly upsetting. When he fell asleep at night, where would his mother be? Not nearby but far away, where he couldn't reach out to her if he needed to. What if his mind started to race as it sometimes did? Who would get things straightened out and help him feel safe again?

The challenges would be, in some respects, enormous. Yet both Pat and Debbie recognized that Sam might be ready. Was it fair to assume the trip was impossible just because Debbie couldn't go? Maybe it was time to give Sam a choice.

They decided to ask him.

Debbie carefully explained the situation to Sam. Why his dad would be going without her. Why it would be impossible for her to get away for the weekend. And then:

"Sam, do you want to go with Mr. Pete? He'll be driving down on Saturday, and you could go with him and then spend Saturday night at the beach with Daddy. It'll be so fun! And I have a lot of work to do. So you'd probably be bored here."

It took Sam a moment to absorb this.

"Mommy, are you going to come later?"

"No, Sam. I wouldn't come. It would just be Daddy."

He thought for a moment. And then he cried. With tears streaming down his face, he nodded. "Yes, I want to go."

Debbie understood his tears. She felt the same way. She wanted to cry, but she wanted Sam to go and have fun and do something she knew he could.

On the Friday before Mr. Pete was to pick up Sam and take him to the shore, Debbie and Sam spent much of the day talking about the trip, event by event. They talked about all of the things he was scared of and what could be done about them. If Sam thought he would miss his mother in the middle of the night and wouldn't know how to find her, then he didn't have to go to bed at all. If he needed to come home, that would be fine. Daddy wouldn't make Sam eat anything he didn't want to eat. Sam could call Debbie at any time. In fact, he could have the telephone right beside him in bed in case he wanted to call her during the night.

On Saturday morning, Sam picked out the clothes he wanted to wear and put them into his little, blue wheeled backpack that had his initials on it. He had a special toiletry bag with his own toothbrush, toothpaste, soap, and shampoo, and he checked it repeatedly to make sure everything was ready to go. The "itinerary" had been reviewed and discussed with his mom. He understood what he could do and whom he might turn to if he was confused, or if things started moving too fast, or if people expected him to do things he couldn't do.

Mr. Pete arrived, and Sam was ready to go. Soon he was buckled into the backseat with the other kids. He waved goodbye to Debbie and—for the first time in his life—headed off to spend a weekend "by himself" at the shore.

Despite thinking about him constantly, Debbie decided not to call him, as she didn't want to interfere with his independent adventure. As it turned out, Pat won his golf tournament and had to attend an awards dinner that evening, which was something they hadn't counted on. But with Mr. Pete's help, Sam took it in stride. Mr. Pete, Howard, and Billy all went to the boardwalk together anyway, and Pat met them there later.

Before Sam went to bed that night, he called his mom and said, "We're having fun, so I'm not coming home tonight. I'm coming home tomorrow."

On Sunday, while Debbie finished up her work, she found herself trying to anticipate what Sam would say when he got back. When the car finally pulled into the driveway and Sam leapt out, the look on his little face told her instantly. It was an expression, Debbie said, that she would always remember.

He rushed into her arms. Debbie said, "Sam, I'm so proud of you!"

"I'm proud of my*self*," he replied. "I'm really proud of myself!"

There, Sam's life changed.

Before that weekend, Sam was a kid who believed that he needed to be near his mother almost constantly, to have her guidance and reassurance as well as her presence. But after that weekend? Sam became a kid who could play on the beach while his mother was far away, and even though it probably made him uneasy, he was able to have a great time, return home, and fling himself into his mother's arms. He became a kid who could feel proud of himself, without needing to be *told* that he was "something else."

Of course, Sam is conscious of none of this, and he is still basically the same kid as before the trip. But in a fundamental way, these tiny steps will take Sam on a journey that is uniquely his own.

I was probably about Sam's age when I first heard the stories of Abraham that my rabbi read from the Bible. From one of those readings, I learned that God had spoken to Abraham and commanded him, "Leave your father's house." Recently I've discovered that there is another, more accurate translation of the words that God spoke to Abraham. In Hebrew, *lech lecha* means "Leave what is familiar"!

God's command was a challenge far more extensive than to leave the house where Abraham and his family lived. God importuned Abraham to leave *everything* that was familiar. He did not tell Abraham to seek wisdom or achieve greatness, but simply to leave. What would happen to Abraham? What happens to each of us? Leaving what's familiar, we enter—

Do you expect me to finish that sentence?

Well, I won't, because I don't know the answer. Perhaps the lesson is that life's journey—the divine journey—is about letting go rather than clinging to the familiar.

Sometimes it's not a choice. Sometimes what is familiar is pulled from our grasp, as in the death of a loved one, divorce, or quadriplegia. But *choosing* to let go of what is familiar is much more difficult in some ways.

⊷⊶

About the time I began this book, I gave up writing a column that had been running every other week for a number of years in the *Philadelphia Inquirer.* I had to struggle with this decision for a long time. The column represented many things to me: a voice in the community, a resource to share what was in my heart and mind. But mostly, it felt like a precious opportunity to talk about what it means to be human, to find compassion for the suffering of others, and to live generously. The column grew in popularity, as did respect and affection for me. To give it up now meant giving up a significant piece of my professional identity, even though the work required more energy than I had. It meant leaving what was familiar. And—it represented a transition from bigger to smaller (whereas Sam's transition was from smaller to bigger).

As I struggled to write my farewell column, I felt a battle going on inside me between my ego and my soul. The ego was saying, "You'll become invisible. You'll no longer have a voice. Your life won't have meaning." In the days following the publication of that column, I lost a great deal of sleep as I mourned what I had given up.

I learned to observe my suffering, and I realized that once I left what was familiar, something unanticipated would take its place. I had faith that no matter what happened, new adventures would await me if I opened to them. Faith that as my life got smaller, I would have many opportunities to experience my life day by day, moment by moment, rather than simply rushing to the next column or lecture.

And the struggle between ego and faith? It felt like a life-or-death conflict, and it truly was. The ego is always fighting for its life, demanding more attention, more wealth, more power and influence. Faith turns its back on the ego and tells us that we are a small part of something larger.

I wrote my last column. I sent it in. And in that final column to my readers, I said:

> All fear is about the future. And when confronted with the fragility of life, it's hard not to think about the future. When we do, however, we are at risk of living in the future. That is the real tragedy, because living in the future takes us away from the life we have today.
>
> I have faced death many times, and I feel my body growing tired. I hope I live another decade or more, but I also know this summer could be my

last. Not that I have a rapidly deteriorating medical condition; I am just fortunate enough to be aware of the fragility of my life. As a result I have discovered that my fear of death wasn't because I didn't want to die. It was because I didn't want to stop living a life I cherish—with all the people I love, the changing seasons, the smell of fresh-cut grass, the sound of the ocean, and my grandson's voice on the telephone saying "Hi, Pop."

My life is not joyous every moment; I still experience the same neurotic anxiety that I always have. But there is also a larger awareness that reminds me that this anxiety or depression or insecurity I might be feeling in any given moment is simply part of the tapestry that is my life. And new emotions and experiences are waiting right around the corner.

Readers who are hoping for a list of practical "tips" of the type we so often see in the news media may be disappointed. I can only offer one big one: Don't spend so much of your energy pursuing the life you want or avoiding the life you fear. Have the faith to live the life you have—and live it fully, with great love and gratitude.

With those words, something ended—a part of the story of who I was and what I could accomplish. Witnessing my own struggle, I became curious. It was interesting to watch this battle between faith and ego, knowing that whatever I'm experiencing today will feel different tomorrow and will be radically different a week from now. I struggle, I suffer . . . and I'm really open.

So I don't think *I'm* sumfing else. But as I think about the journey, the process, the dance between the ego and the soul—that's sumfing else.

જીજી

When we begin to let go of our stories, we actually change ourselves neurologically. Every time we leave behind our habitual thinking and come back to the moment, we begin a process of laying down new pathways in the brain. With enough practice, our brains actually learn that the stories we tell ourselves are just stories that may or may not be valid (usually not, though). Sam can go to the shore by himself now. I can give up my newspaper column. This really is sumfing else. Little Sam will probably move from story to story about himself for the next several decades.

Me? I know that my stories are just stories, and although they help me explain my life, they sometimes prevent me from experiencing it. A Sufi once said: "To explain is to lie, to experience is to live." I've often compared our stories to ships' anchors. They give us a sense of stability in storms, but most of the time, they keep us stuck. Letting go of anything that gives us security or predictability is an act of faith. And having that kind of faith is ultimately the only thing that allows us to feel safe.

જીજી

Oh, and by the way, that column I gave up writing? A couple of months later, an editor at the *Inquirer* asked whether I would be interested in starting a blog where readers and I could correspond regularly. Of course, I said yes.

A new pathway. A new beginning.

CHAPTER 5

I Don't Know
That Face

When I was in college, the Mona Lisa was on a world tour. When she paid a visit to the Metropolitan Museum of Art in New York, my roommate and I decided to go see her. My roommate, an art major, was beside himself with excitement. I wasn't much of an art lover, but I did enjoy having new experiences, so I agreed to go. Although I didn't mind waiting in line all those hours for my friend, I really couldn't understand why so many people wanted to see an old painting.

When I got into the gallery, everything changed. There was something about her face—that expression. I sat on one of those hard benches and stared into the Mona Lisa's eyes until the guards told me I had to leave.

❦❦

In some respects, I have been a student of human nature since I was 12 years old. My classmates trusted me with

THE WISDOM OF SAM

their secrets, and I really valued their trust. Based on that confidence, I thought I had a good ability to "read" what the people around me were thinking and feeling—until the day I saw the Mona Lisa's face.

What *is* her expression? A bit of a smile—most often described as "enigmatic." Dark eyes that almost look straight through you . . . but not quite. She seems slightly distracted, as if she has something on her mind. What is she thinking? Is she just doing her best to look pleasant?

The real beauty of the Mona Lisa—what attracts us— is the way her particular expression opens the door for us to tell any story we want about what she's thinking. Psychologists call that projection. We can attribute any thought or emotion to her and tell ourselves that that was da Vinci's intent, but the story is really our own.

≈⊙⊙≈

Now let's make this more challenging. Suppose you are like Sam and others with autism and have trouble reading people's expressions. Unlike other kids, you don't look at someone who has a big smile and automatically think to yourself, *That person is happy!* The more complex the expression, the more confused you get. When the corners of the mouth go down, the forehead wrinkles, and the eyebrows kind of bunch together over the nose—what does *that* mean? What about clenched teeth, a red face, and a grimace? Especially confusing are subtle expressions like the single arched eyebrow, the furrowed brow, or the shoulder shrug. A kid with autism has a problem reading the expressions of not only total strangers but also the people with whom he's closest—mom, dad, brothers, sisters, grandparents, teachers, and best friends.

Fortunately, therapists who deal with these kids have worked out ways to address this inability to recognize patterns of human expression. As soon as Sam was able to focus his attention on instructional materials, his parents and teachers began showing him illustrations of very distinct expressions—cartoon characters with big smiles or dejected frowns, or subtler expressions that suggested surprise, alarm, or fear. At first the adults had to do a lot of coaching, helping Sam understand that the downturned mouth and tearful eyes meant sadness, or that a wrinkled forehead and upturned eyebrows indicated surprise. Picture books with stories also helped. Teachers could read the story, help Sam interpret the expressions on the faces of the illustrated characters, and then talk about the fear, happiness, anger, or confusion each character in the story might be feeling. In time, Sam learned to do this himself—first with the illustrations and then when he saw comparable visual patterns in people's faces. So he could tell when his mom was wearing her happy face or her sad face. He could make a distinction between those kinds of expressions when they appeared on the faces of his father or his pop or one of his friends.

But there are still some faces that stump him.

One day when Sam was on the swings in the playground, he got pretty exuberant. He started off at a reasonable pace, but as he kicked harder, he started to attain those giddy heights where each plunge—forward or back—is like a brief parachute fall. At those altitudes, of course, a kid begins to imagine spectacular achievements in flight, and any parent begins to imagine equally spectacular disasters.

Debbie was standing nearby.

"Okay, Sam," she said, "that's high enough."

He continued swinging.

"Sam?"

More swinging.

"*Sam!*"

Finally she had his attention. He stopped kicking, slowed, and the swing came to a stop. Debbie got in front of him, crouched down, and looked Sam in the eye.

"That's a little too high, okay? You might fall off, and if you do, you could get hurt." She had his attention. Sam studied his mother's expression.

"Mommy," he said finally. "I don't know that face."

❦

Sam looked at his mother with what the Buddhists call "beginner's mind." He didn't know that face and he knew he didn't understand. And he was comfortable enough to say that. Most of us lose that gentle comfort with our own ignorance when we are still young. As a result, we tend to do with real people what we do with the Mona Lisa. We tell ourselves stories about what they are experiencing, and then we believe those stories. We react to what we think we are seeing, and, inevitably, a drama unfolds.

Of course we are all amateurs when it comes to reading the thoughts and emotions of others, we just don't know it. Sam does.

❦

When Debbie told me about Sam's comment, I immediately flashed back to the months and years right after my accident. When I went into a room or had a new encounter with someone, the first thing I'd look for were the expressions on people's faces. I was too vulnerable and insecure to have a beginner's mind, so when I saw an expression, I would begin telling myself stories. One expression I would read as "Oh, my God, look at that poor crippled man." But there were other days when I read the expressions on people's faces in the opposite way. I would see people who were looking at me with pride and admiration. On bad days, I would see revulsion, and on good days, I would see acceptance. Each one of those stories was about emotions I carried into those encounters.

≪ઈ∕ે≫

Not long ago, a woman called *Voices in the Family* (my public-radio program in Philadelphia) to share a recent incident in her life that had frightened her. The caller had a teenage daughter, and she said she had decided not to tell her daughter how she felt because she didn't want her daughter to know she was scared.

My response was: "Well, good luck with that."

"You mean, you think she'll find out?" the caller asked.

"Or she already knows," I replied.

If I'd had more time with her on the program, I would have told her my story about Debbie's tonsillectomy. When Debbie was four, I took her to the hospital and waited with her before she went in for surgery. Debbie asked if I was worried, and—believing that our children can read us—I tried to be honest. I told her I was worried that the operation might not work and that she would still get a lot of colds. I also said I was worried that it might hurt and that she might be mad at her mom and me for putting her through it.

I tried to explain to Debbie how these were the thoughts running through my head. But of course what I was really trying to do was protect her from my deepest fears. It didn't take long for Debbie to challenge me.

"That's not why you're nervous, Daddy," she said.

"Okay, Debbie, why is Daddy nervous?"

"You're afraid I'm going to die in there. Aren't you?"

Of course she was right. That was the sum of all my fears, but I wasn't even aware of it! I doubt Debbie picked that up from my expression or my words. The fear was in my heart, and somehow she was able to read what was in there.

Now is this just another case of storytelling? Was it really Debbie who was afraid she was going to die and just attributing those feelings to me? Of course that's part of it, but four-year-old Debbie also had a beginner's mind. She knew what she knew and she knew what she didn't know. And she knew her father was feeling great fear.

❧❧

When it comes to reading expressions, I suspect we're all, indeed, somewhere on the spectrum. We do fairly well guessing emotions when we see a truly happy face. We do less well with a happy face that hides a sad face, or an indifferent expression that conceals anxiety, or an angry face that is really fear in disguise. But when we don't know what a face means, do we have beginner's mind, or do we tell ourselves stories?

Most of us grown-ups are in the latter category. We tell ourselves that we know what the other person is feeling, even thinking. Even though we are sometimes right, these are mostly just stories. And then we *believe* the stories, and those stories lead to other stories, and before we know it, we are off in some kind of fictional wonderland.

Sam and most other children have something precious that we have lost. They are comfortable with their own ignorance, so they don't need to make up stories. They have beginner's minds because they are beginners!

So they have the ability to teach us a precious lesson: the gift of looking into someone's eyes and asking what that face means. They are too young to make up stories. And more importantly, they are quite comfortable asking.

CHAPTER 6

Why Do People Have to Get Naked?

When Sam learned "the facts of life," he was eight years old. He'd heard rumors beforehand, and he'd probably picked up the gist from his buddies. But I'm pretty sure his first serious discussion about sex was with me. When he had a visual image of what was involved, he wrinkled his nose. Thereafter, when he referred to sex, it was with this same expression of distaste. He called it "doing that thing." And his big question was, "Why do people have to get naked?"

I think we all have some recollection of how we learned about sex. I was in fifth grade at Granville Avenue School when Fred Nahas told me my parents got naked and had sex. Overcome with embarrassment and anger, I punched him in the face without thinking about how much bigger he was than me. He punched me back, only harder. I could barely move my jaw for the rest of the afternoon and was too embarrassed to tell anyone about it. So my first introduction to sex was pretty painful! And I'm still a little afraid of Fred.

I'm sure you have your own memories of the times when your parents struggled to tell you about sex, or when you finally talked about it with someone you were close to. By seventh grade, I was fine with the idea that people got naked (everyone except my parents) and felt I had a pretty good understanding of sex. I learned a little bit at school, and I learned a lot from my friends and my older sister. But neither of my parents had ever broached the subject with me.

My father was as shy as they come, and he was probably being nagged by my mother to have "the talk" with me. One of them must have realized that my dad would need some textual material to help launch the discussion. I don't know which of them actually bought the how-to book, but one day when I was alone in my room, the door opened a crack and I saw an arm coming in with a book attached to it. I only caught a glimpse of my father's expressionless face as he tossed the book onto my bed and, just as suddenly, closed the door again. The scene was almost like a zookeeper feeding the lions red meat—get in and out as quickly as possible, and avoid any direct contact. Anyway, I opened to the title page and read, *The Facts of Life and Love for Teenagers*.

It was the first time he raised the subject of sex. It would be another 40 years or so before we discussed it again.

ઓજ

Of course, men talk about sex all the time, and as I found out some 30 years later, women are inclined to do the same. Much of the talk among men and boys tends to be quite lewd. It's fairly easy for guys to come up with jokes that work with a male crowd, since most physiological acts, including sex, are rife with comedic material. I'm sure my dad did not hesitate to crack up over rude references when he was with his buddies, and anyone who runs an Army-Navy store is likely to hear more than his share of dirty jokes.

But informing his son about the intimate acts that occurred between his mom and dad, which, by the way, directly caused his birth? Nah, that's far too embarrassing. Toss a book on the kid's bed and quickly close the door!

⊰⊱

When it comes to talking about sex, I learned a valuable lesson from Dr. Jack Friedman, my teacher when I began doing counseling work in family therapy. We were in a session involving a preadolescent girl and her mother. The discussion had reached the point where the adults in the room realized that the girl wanted to know about sex, and the mother was too uncomfortable with the subject to give her the information she needed.

"Would you like me to tell her?" asked Jack.

The mother agreed. Jack proceeded to tell the girl in a detached and dispassionate way about what men and women do: how the sperm fertilizes the egg, how the egg divides, and other basics of the reproductive process. I was drinking all of this in as a future therapist, as a son who didn't have the benefit of such clear information, and as a brand-new father. I was enthralled by the fact that Jack was so calm and instructive. And I watched this young girl absorb the information without expressing discomfort. This was certainly a far cry from my introduction.

The presentation continued for about five minutes, and then there was a pause, after which Jack said something that I will never forget.

"And, by the way, it feels really good."

And I thought, *Nobody ever says that.*

So that taught me how to be honest and clear about sex. But that knowledge didn't make things any easier when I had to talk with my own daughters, especially since they were only five and six years old at the time.

41

My wife, Sandy, and I had just seen the hilarious movie *National Lampoon's Vacation* with Chevy Chase, and we thought most of it would be fine for Ali and Debbie. There seemed to be only one questionable line of dialogue. It occurs when the Griswold family—on their road trip to Wally World—reunite with their crazy, long-lost relatives who have been living in the boondocks. The kids from each family, curious about one another, start talking. The prepubescent Griswold boy, witnessing rural life for the first time, asks his cousin, "What do you do here all day?" To which the older kid replies: "I bop the baloney."

It's a quick line, over in an instant. I thought the girls wouldn't notice, or if they did, there was no way they could interpret what it meant. Sandy was positive they would. In the end, we agreed to disagree and let them see the movie.

The day after the girls watched the movie, when we were all on our way to Sesame Place theme park, I heard some whispering between Debbie and Ali in the backseat. Finally, it was Ali who spoke up.

"Daddy, what does 'bopping the baloney' mean?"

I looked over at Sandy, and she had this awful "I told you so" look on her face. Fumbling for age-appropriate answers, I remembered that when Debbie was little and took baths, she used to like to play with herself. So I reminded Ali about those times and explained that, when boys play with themselves, some say they're bopping the baloney.

This explanation was followed by a few moments of silence. I was just beginning to feel some relief when I heard my child's voice again: "Daddy, when you were a little boy, did *you* bop the baloney?"

Again my stomach was in a knot, and when I looked over, Sandy was actually smiling!

"Well, yes," I responded, "when Daddy was a little boy, he used to bop the baloney."

At that point, I sincerely hoped we'd come to the end of that line of questioning. But of course there was more.

"Daddy," came the voice from the backseat, "do you *still* bop the baloney?"

At that point Sandy actually laughed out loud. I hated her, I hated Chevy Chase, and most of all I hated myself for not listening to Sandy in the first place. Frozen with anxiety, a few seconds later I heard the dreaded question again.

That was it! The line had been crossed and all my inner vows to be honest and forthright with my kids were put on hold. My response was instantaneous.

"Okay, Ali, that's enough! I don't want to talk about this anymore!"

Years later, when, theoretically, I should have felt comfortable talking about sex with my more mature daughters, our conversations were still fraught. By the time the girls were high-school age, Sandy and I had divorced. Sandy, also painfully shy, had never talked to either of them about sex, so I figured that was my duty. I said what I had to. But it was terribly awkward. I remember having a talk with Ali about sex and love and protection and reputation—all the topics I thought were essential. When I was done, Ali turned to me and said, "Dad, I think I have a right to learn this on the street like everyone else." This is the one who had felt it was okay to ask her father if he bopped the baloney!

❧❧

After my mother died, my dad moved to a condominium in Atlantic City where he was surrounded by single widows. More than one of them doted on him. My father—now in his early 80s—told me on the boardwalk one day, "You know, Danny, I'm discovering that I really like girls." When I asked him to define girls, he said, "Women over 70!"

Anyway, I was proud that he eventually mastered the fine art of flirting and found himself in his element. I gave him a hard time because he was having trouble with names and only seemed to remember his ladies by food groups. At one point he was dating three women at once: he just called them nicknames such as sweetie pie, lamb chop, and honey.

He frequently complained that he had no more male friends, so I was the one who got the details of his exploits, which was sometimes far more information than I wanted. One night he called me, quite exhilarated, and said, "Danny, I just got to second base with Sweetie Pie."

"Dad," I said, "I don't even want to know what 'second base' is at your age. I just imagine that it sags closer to home plate. Listen, I'm happy for you, Dad. I love you. But when I picture the two of you at second base, I'm not going to sleep well tonight." We both laughed—that loving father-and-son laugh that we frequently enjoyed together.

So it went, lots of jokes, mano-a-mano, right up until the time Dad had a prostate operation. The surgery left him impotent. That didn't interfere with his flirting, of course, but it was much on his mind.

Several months after the surgery, he came to visit me. I picked him up in my van at the train station, and we headed out along Springdale Avenue toward my house. I asked how things were going. Dad shook his head. "I don't even know why I flirt anymore. I can't even have sex."

I still remember the exact spot on Springdale Avenue where I pulled the van over and came to a stop.

"Dad," I said, "you're telling your *quadriplegic son* you can't have sex because you're impotent?"

"Well," he said, "I never thought of that."

"Right now, you and I are going to have the first sex talk in our lives. And I'm not going to throw any books at you." Remembering Jack Friedman's incredible honesty, I said, "Sex is not as good as it was before. But it's wonderful."

⊰⊱

It was more than a decade later—long after the death of my father—when my grandson began to get curious. Sam asked his mother some questions about the birds and the bees, and she provided the basics. Eventually he came to me and popped the question. "Why do people have to get naked to have sex?" he asked. So, I explained. And he thought it was pretty disgusting.

The topic came up again when my friend Amy had a baby boy. Sam knew Amy quite well, and since he hadn't seen her around in a while, he wondered where she was. I explained that she had just had a baby.

"You mean . . . she did that thing?"

"Yes, Sam," I said. "You know, to an eight-year-old, it's disgusting. But when you're older, it'll be wonderful. You will love a girl in a way that's different from the way you love your mother. Don't worry; it will be a long time before the naked thing becomes an issue. And when that happens, I promise you will be ready. And whenever you want to talk about anything, you'll be able to talk to your mom and your dad and me."

I doubt Sam understood everything I had to say. As a matter of fact, it took me a long time to realize that, ideally, getting naked emotionally is even more intimate than doing it physically. We get naked when we trust the other person with our secrets and vulnerabilities. And sometimes, listening to another person's story is a way of making love. All of the warnings and cautions about sex will wait until he's older. For now, I want him to know that this business is really about love and life.

CHAPTER 7

Everything Just Went Too Fast

I wake up around 6:30 every morning. Even if my body wants to go right back to sleep, my mind gets busy immediately. If you were to eavesdrop on my mental activity, you would find me thinking about my day, or my week, or my trip to California next month. In the opening moments of my day, my mind is already planning.

Then my nurse comes in and begins to help me in the shower. So now I am watching her to make sure all the details of my morning routine get done. While I am in the shower, I am thinking about which clothes I will wear today based on the weather, what appointments I have. All of this occurs while my nurse is washing my body. I may or may not notice the temperature of the water.

After my shower, I am back to observing my nurse. Is she doing my catheter care correctly? Did she remember to unplug my cell phone from its charger? Did she pour the medication correctly? So now my mind goes from planning my future to scanning my environment. However, because

I have a mind that has developed some multitasking skills, I am able to do both. So now I am scanning my environment and thinking about what I want my nurse to make me for breakfast.

When we are done with the morning routine, my nurse puts coffee and the newspaper on the table for me. But what do I do? I quickly shoot into my office to turn on my computer and check my e-mail. Before I know it, I'm lost answering e-mails, checking my schedule, scanning, and planning. From the kitchen comes a voice: "Breakfast is ready!" Usually I hear that voice without *really* hearing it, so about five minutes later I will again hear, "Breakfast is ready!"

After breakfast, I meditate for 30 minutes. Some days, during meditation, I am able to notice my breath and experience my life moment by moment. But on others, I notice my breath, and then a few minutes later, I notice that my attention has been lost in some drama my mind has created. Back to my breath, and then back to planning the future . . .

And this is all before my workday even starts. It happens before I begin researching for my radio show, working on my book, seeing patients, and developing treatment plans. And my poor mind has only been out of bed for two hours!

Then the day begins with appointments, expectations, unreasonable pacing, and typical racing. Though my morning routine differs in its details from yours, I'm sure you can identify. We go through our days often without even noticing what this pace is doing to us. We don't notice the cortisol and adrenaline coursing through our veins, making our hearts race faster. We don't notice the tension in the neck or stomach. Usually, we don't notice the racing mind.

∽∾

Sam does.

It was the summer of the sixth year of his life, and his pop had come to visit for the weekend. On this particular Saturday, Sam wanted to show me how I could play tennis with him on his Wii and how he had just learned to ride a two-wheeler. And his mother wanted to make a big breakfast before we all left, at 11:00 A.M., for his T-ball game. So we hurried through everything to get to the game on time. I could see Sam getting frustrated with the way the day was unfolding.

And it got worse. After the T-ball game, some guests arrived at the house, and things became pretty hectic. It was obvious that Sam's frustration was building. He was getting overstimulated, and it showed in his rapid breathing and darting eyes. When Sam was about two, he would get down on all fours and bang his head against the floor when he felt this way. Now his body just went rigid and he started screaming.

Sam insisted everyone leave the room except Debbie and Pop. Then he screamed until he collapsed on the floor and started to sob. Debbie held him until he was done sobbing.

Eventually he looked up and said, "Mommy, everything just went too fast inside my head today."

∽⩔⩔

How many of us could say that?

I've described what a morning is like for me, so, obviously, there are times (okay, every day) when everything just goes too fast inside my head, too. I wish I could feel it every time it happens, but I don't.

Learning how to cope with the anxiety and distress that, for many, begin in early childhood is a normal and healthy part of human development. So the mind races every now and then when stress increases. No big deal.

But many children grow up in high-achieving households where there is sustained anxiety. Sadly, the number of children who suffer from childhood anxiety disorders and depression is on the rise, especially in upper-middle-class families. Suniya Luthar, Ph.D., of Columbia University has published several studies showing that adolescent girls who grow up in families earning just over $100,000 are twice as likely to have depression and three times as likely to have anxiety disorders as girls who grow up in families that are less well-off.

When a child is exposed to frequent anxiety or volatility, his instinct is to work very hard to stabilize the environment so he feels safe. These children often become overachievers or caretakers. In my practice, when I observe spouses trying to change one another, I feel like I am watching childhood dramas being reenacted as these two adults try to create an environment that will make them feel safe and secure.

And it's not just them. In today's world, without even knowing it, we push ourselves to find that holy grail—that thing we call security or stability, that thing that we hope will lead us to happiness. Unfortunately, we rarely find that at the end of the day, or week, or year, so we try even harder and race even faster.

Meanwhile, not only are we failing to stabilize our environment but we are also feeling more stress and insecurity because it's the pursuit itself that is causing most of our stress. And what our body, our brain, and our spirit really need is for everything to stop going so fast inside our heads. In times like these, the soul only needs one thing—quiet. Our brains need respite, but our minds are racing too fast to realize it.

In a way, we are all sleepwalking through our lives. I recently gave a lecture on stress to medical students at grand rounds. When I suggested that they try taking a few minutes several times a day to simply breathe and feel, most argued that they just didn't have time. So I asked them to do one tiny thing for themselves. "When you put your hand on a doorknob to visit with a patient," I said, "simply feel the temperature of the doorknob. Just pay attention to that moment, and be aware of your life."

When we're sleepwalking, we abandon our experience. Often if I find my mind racing in the middle of the day when I am trying to concentrate, I'll just stop and breathe for a few minutes, simply noticing what I'm feeling. And often what I discover are feelings I was not aware of just a few minutes earlier. Sometimes I feel exhaustion or frustration. On rare occasions, I feel anger—though far more typically it's anxiety. But whatever the emotion, I simply let myself feel what I feel without having to do anything about it, without having to fix anything so that I no longer feel it.

Sounds simple—but when I am able to do that, somehow I find myself returning to the experience of my life. So rather than trying to push myself harder to manage my anxiety, I do what is counterintuitive: I stop and just feel my life for a few minutes. It's not always pleasant, and sometimes it can be pretty *unpleasant,* but it always feels better than it does when my mind is racing and I am not awake to my experience.

◈◈

I'd like to invite you to do something different. Check in with yourself three or four times a day and ask simply: "How are you?" Then pause for just a few minutes, feel your breath, and begin to answer that question. If your mind is racing, that means your heart is closed and you need compassion. Nothing dramatic, just to observe yourself as you would observe someone you adore—and feel compassion for that person who has a racing mind and closed heart. Try it. The entire exercise shouldn't take more than five minutes.

Now perhaps you feel a bit calmer. And you might even feel the emotion that often follows. Sam does. Two years after Sam's incident, I reminded him of his words and asked him whether there were still times when everything just went too fast inside his head.

"Not that often," Sam replied. "It used to happen more when I was little."

"Is it scary when it happens?" I asked.

"No, just upsetting."

"Does it make you mad?"

Sam thought about that for a moment.

"Mostly sad," he said.

∽๑๑∾

I invite you to put this book down for a minute. Notice whether your heart is open or closed. Notice whether your mind is racing or your muscles are tense. As you settle in and observe how hard your mind and body are working, perhaps, like Sam, you might feel sadness, too.

But whatever you feel, as long as you are able to notice your mind with genuine curiosity, and maybe even some compassion for that mind that works so hard, you will have found the place where everything stops moving so fast.

CHAPTER 8

Toughen Me Up

For the first time in over 20 years, I was about to make the train trip from Philadelphia's 30th Street Station to Union Station in Washington, D.C., to meet with a magazine editor. Debbie and Sam would meet me at Union Station, where we would all have lunch before I went to my appointment.

Before my accident, I wouldn't have thought twice about the difficulties associated with this train ride. Thirty years ago, I would have driven to 30th Street, parked my car, walked to the station, bought a ticket, checked the departure board, bought a cup of coffee, walked downstairs to the platform, found a seat, put my briefcase on the overhead rack, and settled in for the ride. Easy.

But that was then. Now I was confined to an electric wheelchair. I could drive my van to the station, but would I be able to find handicapped parking near the entrance? And if there was a space, would it have the eight feet of clearance on the side of the van that I needed for my ramp extension? I could preorder a ticket online so that I would be guaranteed a space to park my wheelchair on the Metroliner, but how would I access the platform? Would there be an elevator, and if so, would it be working? Once I made it to the platform, how big would the gap between the platform and the train be? And once on board, would I be able to maneuver the sharp turn to get into the car? Would there be anyone around to help me? Did Amtrak have a way to notify the people in Union Station that I would be arriving so they could make the necessary arrangements?

I did as much research and preparation as I could, but many of these questions would not be answered until I got there. "Handicap accessible" is a convenient turn of phrase, but in my three decades of experience driving a wheelchair, I've learned to plan for the worst. Too often, elevators don't work, or they've been so neglected they get stuck. I've encountered innumerable blocked entryways. Ramps so steep that my chair would tip over backward. Turns so tight that finding a way out is like unlocking a Chinese puzzle. Not to mention all the risks of mechanical stalemate if my chair gets damaged, if the batteries fail, the lift malfunctions, or my catheter tube comes loose and I wet my pants. Or the physical risks of getting too hot or too cold (I can't tolerate temperature extremes for long), of a blood-pressure spike, of dehydration.

It would be the first time since my accident that I would be taking the train. I would be doing it by myself. And I was scared.

That train ride was a leap of faith. And sure enough, there were difficulties: finding a parking space for the van, negotiating the tight turns when I got on the train. At the other end, in Union Station, the only way to get up off the platform was by means of a flimsy little aluminum lift that felt like it would collapse. But I made it. I felt pride in what I had done and then, when Debbie appeared, relief mingled with joy. My relief was not just in getting there but also, having found Debbie, feeling that I was safe in her care. Now, if anything happened, I wouldn't be alone.

And there was Sam, fresh from wrestling practice, still in his little uniform with the bright colors and the muscle-man top. He was excited to see me and alert to all the sights and sounds of the enormous station. As we headed toward the restaurant, with Sam freeloading a ride on the back of my chair, I could tell that he had something on his mind.

◈◈

That was near the end of Sam's first season at the Boys Club when he was wrestling against other six-year-olds. And Sam had a very special coach. A wrestler in high school, Pat had volunteered to be the kids' instructor. So Sam's dad was teaching him to wrestle!

Even with the six-year-old group, wrestling practices run more than an hour, and each one is a real workout. The boys do calisthenics and stretches, and then practice different repetitive moves. Pat likes to keep the boys concentrated and serious, but they always end with something fun—a game that involves group participation. At the conclusion of each session, he gives a short inspirational talk about wrestling etiquette, or eating the right foods and staying in shape, or the importance of practice.

From Pat, I knew that wrestling didn't come naturally to Sam. He was an enthusiastic participant in all the practices, okay with calisthenics, and attentive when he was being taught. The part he didn't get was why one kid would aggressively attack another. That puzzled Sam. Why would someone try to hurt him? Some of the other six-year-olds— especially the boys who were used to duking it out with their brothers at home—would jump right in and wrestle aggressively. Sam wasn't like that. He seemed perplexed that anyone would intentionally try to knock him down and possibly hurt him. Don't get me wrong, he has all the testosterone of an average boy and likes to play rough-and-tumble, but the idea of hurting another person is pretty alien to him.

For a while, Debbie was allowed to attend the practices, but with the strict instruction not to interfere. Predictably, she soon broke the rule. When Sam got his first bloody nose during a match, Debbie could not help rushing to his side to comfort him and wipe up the blood. In so doing, she embarrassed her son as well as his coach. After that, Debbie was banned from the sidelines!

She did go to tournaments, however, and so I became familiar with Sam's wrestling record. That first year was pretty uncomplicated. He lost every match.

To Sam's great credit, the loss at the tournament and the defeats during matches in practice did not dim his enthusiasm. He loved the sport and loved having his father as coach. As for Pat, he treated Sam like all the other kids. Apart from that one episode when Debbie was barred from the premises, Sam had never received any special attention.

Of course, as far as Pat was concerned, it didn't matter whether Sam won or lost as long as he continued to be interested and engaged. Despite Sam's lack of natural aggressiveness, Pat noticed one thing that was in Sam's favor. Once Sam caught on to a move and understood what it was for, he was precise about repeating it. Pat didn't know how much Sam's compulsive attention to detail was connected to his autism, but as long as Sam continued to practice and learn the responses he needed for each situation, that ability could—in time—make up for his lack of aggression.

From my own conversations with Sam, I knew he was not very upset about losing the practice matches against the other kids in his group. He did not seem particularly deterred by the aggressiveness of the other kids—just puzzled. But I knew he was competitive. And I wondered whether he was hiding his disappointment.

As we sat in the restaurant and ordered our lunch, Sam and I caught up on recent events. Many of my questions had to do with wrestling, and when the conversation turned in that direction, despite knowing the answer, I asked him how it was going. I could see that troubled look on his face. "I've lost all of my matches so far, Pop." Sam is small for his age, so I wondered if he was wrestling against larger children his age and asked him whether that was a factor. But he explained very matter-of-factly that all of the kids he wrestled were his size.

"So, Sam, why do you think you've lost all your matches?"

He was quiet for a few minutes, and then, as though he had found the exact reason, he said: "I don't think I am tough enough." After a brief pause, he added, "Pop, Mom told me you used to wrestle in high school. Do you think you could toughen me up?"

"Sure, Sam," I replied, "I'll help toughen you up."

✎✐

Fortunately, the first step had already been accomplished: Debbie had been banned from the practice room. If I had been at those practices with her, I would have been happy to tell her that Sam didn't need his mother. I doubt she would have listened to me, though. The real message is a difficult one. Debbie had to step aside and allow her son to get his nose bloodied, his knees scraped, and even his butt kicked every now and then. That's more reality than most moms want to witness. Certainly, in Debbie's case, it violated all her protective instincts. And Debbie's protective instincts may be even more powerful than most. Debbie has her own anxiety (some of it genetic and some the result of a difficult childhood), but any parent of a child who is somehow more vulnerable than others is going to be especially protective, if not overprotective. Nevertheless, a child's growth requires parents to release their protective grasp. Once Debbie left the practice room, Sam had the opportunity to learn that he could face adversity on his own terms. So Pat and Sam had already taken care of the protective mom. What else could *I* do to toughen Sam up the way he wanted to be?

Although I had wrestled in high school, I had been even less successful than Sam. Not only did I not have the aggressive instinct, I lacked the commitment to learn this new craft. As a result, I got my butt kicked at least twice a week. When it finally dawned on me that I wasn't enjoying it, I quit. And nothing in my recent experience had made me any more of an expert at wrestling. Let's face it, there is a reason why there are no quadriplegic wrestling teams—a quadriplegic wrestling match would be pretty boring! So I couldn't be a wrestling teacher, but I could still offer advice about toughening up.

∞∞

When I was growing up in Margate, New Jersey, my backyard had the reputation of being the finest wiffleball field in town. The home-run marker was a slatted fence about five feet high, located a hundred feet from home plate. When I was about Sam's age, I was playing in the backyard by myself. At one point I climbed to the top of that fence, stood up, lost my balance, and fell on the ground face first. I had the wind knocked out of me and was in a great deal of pain, but no one was around.

To this day I remember lying on the ground. For the first time in my life, I didn't cry. Not only that, I didn't seek help, and I didn't tell anyone what had happened. I quickly realized that the event wasn't that important. I remember feeling exhilarated, knowing that I could handle pain. Though I didn't have the language to say what I'd learned, I later understood that I had had my first experience with resilience. I had begun to develop faith that I could get hurt and still be okay.

When I fell off the fence, I felt pain. But for the first time, I didn't suffer. In hindsight, that was my first lesson in the difference between pain and suffering. It would take me at least another 40 years to really understand that lesson!

That's what Sam needed. He needed to learn that pain is pain and doesn't necessarily need to be fixed; that 99.9 percent of the time, pain heals on its own; and that more often than not, trying to fix pain actually makes it worse. That's because when we wrap our minds around the pain and try to fix it, all we are really doing is holding on to it. We talk about the experience, who caused it, the injustice, our indignation. During the popular-psychology movement of the '70s, many of us were told we should "get rid of it" by venting or blowing off steam. That usually doesn't work. In fact, venting actually makes the pain worse because the more we talk about it and think about it, the longer the pain stays with us. And that is when pain turns into suffering.

When I fell off the fence, I learned I was okay. More importantly, I had faith that if it happened again, as it surely would, I would again be okay.

What Sam needed was trust that he had the resilience, in himself, to meet the unknown, to experience it, and to survive. He needed to learn the lessons that only nature—not his parents—could teach him. What he needed from his mom and dad was what all children need from their parents: the faith that they can endure adversity. When a child does not have a parent's faith, he experiences the parent's anxiety. And in time, that child comes to experience himself as fragile in the face of a difficult world. As a result, he never gets a chance to "toughen up."

So I told Sam about the train trip I had just taken. My anxiety beforehand. My distress when things were going wrong. My realization that things would happen that I couldn't control. I told him that even grown-ups have these feelings, but that, deep down inside, I knew that no matter what happened that day, I would be okay. I knew that if something happened, I would be able to ask for help, and I'd be able to figure out what I needed. So at the deepest levels, I had faith in my resilience.

I didn't need to tell Sam what he needed to win matches. He'd already figured that out for himself. Sam had an almost Buddha-like wisdom to assess his own situation. He was able to stand outside himself and figure out what the problem was. Because he was able to see himself objectively (without beating himself up), he was able to decipher what he needed. What he was asking for—that quality he called toughening up—was really resilience.

When Sam asked me to toughen him up that day, his request made me think of the ethical will. In Hebrew teachings, the ethical will is described as the responsibility we all share to tell our progeny the wisdom we've acquired and how we acquired it. But there's no way I can teach Sam how to be resilient. That's something he already has inside. It just needs to be nurtured by faith.

I don't know about you, but all the wisdom I've acquired has come from adversity, pain, suffering, loss, and some really stupid decisions. All of these things have caused me great suffering. I have learned that every time I suffer, I recover. And over time, that knowledge has turned to faith. Now I have faith that when I face adversity, somehow I'll be okay. It might not be the outcome I would prefer, but I have faith that I will be okay with what is.

Bouncing back can be pretty easy, and Sam has already demonstrated that. But my great wish for him is that he may have faith that he will be okay. Life will toughen him up. Faith will open his heart.

CHAPTER 9

My Kind of Place

I wonder who first asked a child, "What do you want to be when you grow up?" It's not the kind of question that kids ask themselves—at least not when they're small. They're more curious about "What am I going to get for breakfast?" or "Do bugs have mothers?" or "When is my friend coming over?" They're not concerned with "What will I *be*," much less the remote concept of "growing up." If children thought about what they wanted to be when they grew up, they might say they wanted to be grown-ups so they could eat candy whenever they wanted. They aren't focused on creating a résumé that tells them who they are.

That question also reveals a lot about our own projections. When we lecture people about setting their sights on a worthy goal, we are often talking to ourselves. The reason one of our earliest questions to our child is "What do you want to be?" is because most of us can't answer it for ourselves.

Of course, we think we can. We think we know who we should be, and many adults devote their lives to the cause of trying to become those people. We choose a career or profession and try to excel. We look for a partner or spouse, and then that person becomes part of our identity. We follow a religion or set of beliefs and begin to identify with those of the same persuasion. All of this is part of a process that might be called "finding ourselves." So when we turn to a child and say, "What do you want to be when you grow up?" it's asked with the assumption that he or she will be going through a similar process. The answer we're looking for is, "I want to be a [fill in the profession, aspiration, or achievement]." As in, "I want to be a doctor," "I want to be president," or "I want to fly to Mars."

Eventually some of those identifying markers are achieved. I did what was necessary to become a psychologist. I fell in love with a woman who became my wife. Later I became a father. I became a quadriplegic. I became a teacher, a talk-show host, an author, and a grandfather. But are any of these who I am?

～❦～

On an autumn day when Sam was about six years old, he was helping his father rake leaves in the backyard. Of course a boy of six isn't much help in the leaf-raking department, but he had a little rake of his own and for a while he mimicked his father's industrious strokes. It was a warm day and there were plenty of distractions—darting squirrels, odd-shaped twigs and branches, and an infinite array of brightly colored leaves. Still, Sam remained industrious for quite a while.

The pile of leaves kept growing until it formed one huge, fluffy, multicolored mound. The attraction was too much for Sam. He tossed aside his rake, ran into the pile, sank in deeply, and rolled on his back. Pat came over to have a look. Sam was motionless, looking up through the dappled sunlight to the tops of the trees. And as his father approached, he heard Sam's private musing.

"Now," Sam was saying, "*this* is my kind of place."

࿊

Tell me you don't envy Sam. The warm autumn day. The soft, forgiving pile of leaves. The bliss of nowhere to go, nothing to do—just to lie there knowing this place, the place you occupy at this moment, is your kind of place.

Stop doing what you are doing for the moment and observe your life. Whether you are jumping in the leaves or raking them, whether you are talking with someone you love or reading a book, just experience your place. Can you forget, just for the moment, the task or the outcome or even the process and just experience who you are right now? Sam can, but soon there will be social pressure for him to "behave more responsibly." Just like that question about what he would like to be, he will be told that what he does leads to what he will become. Don't get me wrong, outcome is important. We have to be responsible parents, wage earners, and all that. But perhaps outcome is not as important as we think it is.

Sam knows that. He knows that where he is right now is exactly where he belongs. And like most children, he knows things we have long since forgotten.

࿊

When I was in graduate school in 1969, one of my classes was in existential psychology. At the time, I was too young and immature to realize what an interesting topic this was. I just thought it was a bunch of meaningless philosophical babble. On the day I'm remembering, I was unprepared (not an unusual occurrence). So when the teacher pinned her gaze on me and asked, "Daniel, do I exist?" I had no idea how to answer the question. So I blurted out the first thing that came to mind: "Who wants to know?"

That comeback, I was sure, would get me thrown out of the class. To my astonishment the teacher thought it was brilliant.

When an adult asks a child what she wants to be when she grows up, the adult wants to know. But when an adult asks himself the same question—well, who *does* want to know?

Most humans have an internal judge. You know, the voice that says you are not good enough, or people will laugh at your presentation, or if you don't do something right away, your children will fail in life. That voice that seems to be with us all the time. That's the voice that says you are not quite who you should be. So who is that voice? Who really does want to know? Most of us listen to that voice as though it were the voice of truth. The fact is it is probably the voice of anxiety. Whenever I find myself passing judgment, I see that voice as a scared child biting his nails, saying, "Maybe if we do this, then the anxiety will go away." Of course it never does. And it's also not a great idea to listen to the voice of an anxious child.

So who wants to know? Wouldn't it be great if that voice we had inside of our heads was compassionate and reassuring? Imagine if that voice were to tell us, "Where you are right now is where you belong."

<hr/>

Not long ago I had some sessions with Mathilde, the head of an academic department at a large university. Because of university politics, she had lost her position as chairman and was now doing research full-time. Additionally, her youngest daughter had recently left for college. Mathilde had always felt good about the way she balanced her career and motherhood, so without being aware of it, she had come to define herself as a respected department chair and a loving mother. That's who she was. And now both roles were gone. Laced with the grief of these significant losses were the existential questions: "Who am I now? What should I be doing with the rest of my life?" And underlying all of this anxiety, the universal question: "What will become of me?"

Whenever we feel vulnerable, this question arises. This existential anxiety often forms the underpinnings of dysthymia (mild depression) and nonspecific anxiety disorders. Mathilde experienced it as an identity crisis. She assumed that if she worked hard and found her new identity, the anxiety would go away.

She asked me, "Have you ever had an identity crisis?"

I had to answer, "Sure, I've had them off and on my whole life."

And it's true. Like everyone else, I've spent years trying to find an identity that would feel right and make me comfortable with who I am. And at different stages I have. I discovered a sense of comfort associated with those identities . . . and then they passed or evolved.

So, like everyone else, I'm part of various groups— my community; my family; my profession; my racial, economic, and religious groups. But even though I "belong" to those groups, none of them is more important than any other, and my belonging does not define who I am. Take my family, for instance. When I meet up with my cousins at an occasional reunion, I can look around and say, "I'm *like* them, but I'm *different* from them." I see the family resemblances and connections, but no one else there is a psychologist, or quadriplegic, or an author. More importantly, no one else there thinks like I do or sees the world like I do. I've had this experience with my family my whole life, but when I was younger I thought there was something wrong with me and that I should think the same as everyone else in my family.

As I got older, my position felt lonely. And now, over time, I have reached a point where it mostly feels liberating. Sometimes I am sad and lonely, but usually the feeling of difference gives me the freedom to be who I am—to know that *who* I am and *where* I am is right where I belong. Now it feels comfortable, like some simple truth that I no longer have to struggle with.

When I told Mathilde I had struggled with identity most of my life, she asked if I had ever *found* my identity.

"No," I replied. "I never did. I just stopped looking because it doesn't feel so important anymore, and that feels much better."

≼ઉૐ≽

In a previous book, I wrote about the time shortly after my accident when I was trying to decide whether or not to commit suicide. I chose to live because I told myself that my children needed me, my wife needed me, and my patients needed me. Many of us get our identities, our sense of importance, from the thought that people or events are dependent on us—that we are indispensable. Another illusion. As Yitzhak Rabin once said, "The cemetery is full of people who were indispensable."

This is what Mathilde was facing. She had felt indispensable as a mother. Then her daughter went away to college and, as it turned out, was doing just fine without her. Mathilde held an important academic position, but she knew, just as certainly as her daughter could get along without her, so could the university. When she retired, she would be replaced.

I learned that same lesson right after my accident. Before then, I was a busy professional, running two outpatient drug treatment clinics in West Philadelphia and managing an inpatient detox unit, with a host of related responsibilities. I was supervising more than 20 people and treating about the same number of patients. But then came the accident. I left, without advance notice, for over a year. Everything kept functioning without missing a beat.

Like Mathilde, these pieces of my identity were illusions. So who am I? Who was she? And who wants to know?

The question is no longer who I am; the question is only about what I contribute while I am here. You see, who I am is really about how I live. And I wish to live fully awake and alive, experiencing my life as it comes. The quality of our lives is not about what we possess or what we have achieved, it is about what we have let go.

∽৯৹৵

Before long, Sam will be dealing with these issues in his own way. Already, at the age of eight, he's just beginning to think about who he is and why. Everything he does—like sleeping away from his mom for the first time—helps him to define his selfhood. As he goes through life, I hope he will try on many identities.

But while all that identity-seeking is going on, I hope he doesn't lose what he already has—the ability to live fully awake and alive, experiencing his life. I know he has that ability. After all, that pile of leaves is his kind of place.

CHAPTER 10

Enough Madness

One evening during dinner, Debbie put creamed spinach on Sam's plate. He eyed it suspiciously. He sniffed it. He poked at it. And finally he worked around it.

"Come on, Sam," Debbie prompted. "Try it. Daddy likes it. Mommy likes it. You won't know whether you like it or not unless you try it."

"No, I don't like it."

"You haven't even tasted it yet!"

"It smells funny."

"It just smells different. That's because you haven't tried it before."

"I don't like it."

"You can't say you don't like it if you haven't tried it."

"I don't need to."

"Yes, you do."

"No, I don't."

And the debate continued until it was—as is so often the case in such situations—a battle of wills. The well-meaning mom, at the end of a long day, faced with the obstinacy of a child who refuses to have anything to do with a food of suspicious origins. A food that smells strange. That has the wrong texture. That presumes to occupy a position on his plate where it clearly doesn't belong.

Until, finally, Sam put down his fork. He raised his hands to his cheeks and began shaking his head.

"Mommy," he declared, "I don't like my dinner! That's *enough madness* for one night!"

And with that, he left the table.

This all took place at dinnertime. But I'm sure the real story began much earlier. On Sam's side, it was a school day fraught with all the anxiety of riding the bus with other kids, dealing with adults who kept wanting him to do things. Perhaps a teacher gave an assignment he wasn't expecting, or someone moved his backpack when he wasn't looking. Once home, I expect that he (like most humans) thought he was safe at last, in an environment where everything had its place and his mother could anticipate his needs. And instead, he found *this* on his plate—a strange-smelling, oddly textured mess of something that was sickly green and pasty white.

And Debbie? I don't know for certain, but given her usual day I would guess that she had dealt with dozens of e-mails and phone calls at work. I'm sure she had shopping to do, meetings to arrange, perhaps a consultation with a teacher or advisor—all on a tight schedule that dictated she get home before Sam arrived. I don't know how she felt that evening, but I can say with great confidence that on a different day, Debbie would not have nagged Sam to eat his creamed spinach. I have observed instances where she would use smooth and creative ways to introduce him to something new. Or times when she would be fine letting him choose what he wanted to eat and leave the rest. So why, today, did she nag him? Well, maybe Debbie had her own madness that day. Maybe Debbie's anxiety was higher that day. Maybe her sense of comfort with herself and the world was lower that day. Maybe she was tired, or hungry, or irritated with something that had happened earlier.

For whatever reason, on that particular evening, what Debbie saw as a necessity was, to Sam, pure madness. And of course when Sam talks about madness, he's talking about anger. He was angry at his mother, his situation, and who knows what else.

❦

It has been said that anger is a judicial emotion—a reaction to injustice. Think about your own moments of anger—when someone cuts you off on the highway, or you're on hold for 30 minutes waiting for a customer service representative, or your spouse is not home when he or she is supposed to be there. Most of us get angry when these things happen because they feel like injustices. What's happening is *just not fair!* Whenever we see outrage—whether it is in ourselves or on the world stage—it's about perceived injustice. And most arguments are about fighting for fairness.

In Sam's case, his refusal was not simply based on his dislike for creamed spinach. It was a cry against injustice. At a deeper level, Sam knew what he wanted. He wanted safety and respite from a stressful day. He also knew what he *didn't* want. And here was a person of power—a person he loved and wanted to please—asking him to do what he didn't want to do.

❦

We all experience injustice. When we do, we feel shame, hurt, or fear. Those are our first reactions. But within milliseconds comes the secondary emotion, anger, which protects us from feeling the helplessness and vulnerability that lie beneath our anger. Our instinct is to get retribution or to withdraw. When people hurt us for some unknown or inexplicable reason, we want to hurt them back. Or run away to escape the threat, as I wanted to do when the doctors tried to shave my beard.

It was about a week after my accident, and I had been told that I would need surgery to fuse my vertebrae to avoid further damage to my spinal cord. The surgeon would have to go in through the front part of my neck. The night before surgery, a nurse's aide came into my room with a shaving kit. When I asked, "What's that?" She said, "We have to shave your beard off before surgery."

I snapped. "I will lie in this bed and *die* before you will shave my beard!"

I can still remember the look on her face. How could she begin to imagine what I was feeling at that moment? During this first week after I broke my neck, when I was lying in bed immobilized, I had been visited daily by doctors telling me what I would have to deal with for the rest of my life. They talked about skin breakdowns (bedsores) on my buttocks that could only be treated by going to bed and not sitting in my wheelchair. They discussed urinary-tract infections, blood-pressure fluctuations, spasms, and the sexual ramifications of high spinal-cord injury. These, they explained, were just some of the things I would have to endure. The more I heard, the more I felt out of control of my life and my body. Every day brought another loss, another injustice.

Shaving my beard was the final straw. I'd worn it since I was 18 years old. Everything else had been taken from me, but they weren't going to take my beard.

The nurse's aide called in the head nurse. "You're not shaving it," I repeated. The head nurse called her supervisor.

The supervisor paged the resident on call. The resident called the staff doctor at home. Each of them tried to persuade me that surgery would be impossible unless they shaved off my beard. Each heard the same response from me. They could shave my beard when I was dead. Then, and only then.

Enough of the madness.

In the end, we managed to reach a compromise. They shaved off one side of my beard—enough to allow the surgeon to do what he had to do—and I kept the rest.

But of course it had never been about the beard in the first place. It had all been about the injustice.

❧❧

When I recall the expression of confusion and anxiety on the face of that nurse's aide who bore the brunt of my anger, I wonder how things could have been different. What if I'd had the ability to tell her, or her supervisors, or any of those visiting doctors how I was feeling? What if someone had listened? Not one of those doctors had ever asked me, "What's it like?" If one of them had, I'm sure I would have started to cry—and perhaps never stopped.

So what do we really need in the face of injustice? Like I said, there's a part of our brain that reacts by seeking revenge or retribution, which is how our legal system has evolved. And when we think about most global conflicts, their source is invariably a reaction to injustice or fear of injustice. In the face of injustice, we want what we've lost, whether it is our dignity, our sense of security, a lover, or our health. But we never get what we've lost, and we rarely heal from the injustice even if we do obtain some form of retribution. That's why when perpetrators go to prison, victims might feel a sense of relief or revenge, but rarely do they feel as though a wound has been healed.

So how do we heal? What we really need in the face of injustice is not retribution, but restoration. Restorative justice took place at the Truth and Reconciliation Commission hearings in South Africa. Victims of apartheid got to tell their stories to the perpetrators. The perpetrators listened, and healing began. And now restorative justice programs are taking place all over the world, including in many American prisons.

When we have faced injustice, healing cannot take place until we can tell our story to the person who harmed us. And telling that story is an act of courage because it inevitably involves loss, hurt, and shame. If I could have told my doctors the extraordinary anguish and fear I felt, and if they could have listened with an effort to understand my suffering . . . well, if all of that could have happened, I would have felt less alone in this world. I would have felt less powerless and more connected. And perhaps then, I could have begun to feel some understanding and compassion toward those who hurt me.

If Sam had been able to turn to his mother and tell her what it was like to meet creamed spinach at the end of the day he had just lived through, he would still have felt hurt and wounded but he probably wouldn't have been overwhelmed by the madness.

CHAPTER 11

How You Back Today, Mommy?

Some time ago, I paid a visit to my dentist's office, where I was treated by the dental hygienist. She was a woman her late 20s whom I'd never met before. I told her I'd lost a cap from one tooth. It wasn't painful, but it needed attention.

During the next half hour or so, the hygienist prepared my tooth so the cap could be reattached, and we had some time to talk. Between the flossing, picking, polishing, and rinsing, I found out that her mother had died when she was young. She told me that for a while after her mother's death, she had become quite close to her father until he remarried and started a new family. After that, she said, she began to feel rejected, as most of her father's attention went to the children in his new marriage.

As the hygienist continued working, she told me more about herself—how she and her fiancé had recently bought a condominium, then decided to sell it and move in with his parents so that she could continue her education and get to the next level in her profession. She told me how wonderful her in-laws had been to her.

As it turned out, capping my tooth was indeed a simple procedure.

Before I left, I told her that she had made my day. She thanked me. "You made my day, too," she said.

≪ঌ৵≫

So that was my visit to the dentist. But even as I'm recounting it, I'm leaving out the part that's most difficult to describe. The more I listened, the more I felt attracted to her. Although she was an adorable young lady with a big bright smile, dark wavy hair, and sparkling eyes, I wasn't attracted to her physically. It was something else. Something about this young woman's tenderness made me want to know more and to care deeply about her. I left that office with a wonderful, loving feeling—with a tender, open heart. And even though I may never see her again, I felt connected, like I had another person in my life whom I cared about, and as a result, my world became bigger.

In truth, I have no idea what our interaction meant to her (though I have tried to imagine it), but I know what it was for me. I wasn't just uttering a platitude when I told her she had made my day. I said it with all sincerity. As for her reply—it seemed just as sincere. Whatever the depth of that connection, I know that, for that time, we were both very present in each other's lives.

When I try to imagine living in a different kind of world, one without those connections, I simply can't fathom it. I don't understand how we would survive. And yet this seems to be what's happening in our society. Studies show that people in our culture are increasingly isolated, and technology is making things worse. Twenty years ago, most Americans could say they had four "intimate friends." Today, that number has diminished to three. These statistics make me quite sad and concerned. If things continue this way, teeth will be cleaned, but will stories be told and hearts be opened?

∽⟨⟩∾

When I first learned that Sam had a pervasive developmental disorder, I wondered what he might miss. What emotions would he be incapable of feeling? If he couldn't read facial expressions, did that also mean that he would be unable to recognize his own heart's promptings— messages of joy, sorrow, love, and all the rest? Would the articulation of feelings be entirely beyond his grasp? Would he be able to recognize the connection between his own feelings and those of others? Would his rigid need for orderliness be so all-consuming that he would have to block out his awareness of anyone else?

Empathy and compassion have been important forces in my life, critical to my survival. I was troubled by the possibility that they would be beyond Sam's reach. What would life be like for him if he could not feel that connection to others? For me, such a life would be heartless—a mechanical process of getting along, taking care of business, watching the days pass. It would be like a visit to the dentist's office where there was no young woman with a kind heart and a gentle touch.

Was that what lay ahead for Sam?

He was almost four years old before I had my answer.

That was Sam's age when he started to put sentences together. Though he had been going to a preschool where he had the guidance of wonderful teachers and speech therapists, he had only recently begun to speak, and his language skills were still behind those of many other kids his age. Even so, his parents and I were thrilled at the progress he had made. With each visit, I could see improvements in his ability to express himself. Sam wasn't necessarily proud of himself for being able to speak, it just seemed natural. Soon he was able to tell us what was on his mind. And by age four, he had begun to ask questions.

This was around the time when Debbie was dealing with an extraordinary amount of back pain. An MRI showed a bulging disk, but neither rest nor benign neglect (treatments of choice for most disk problems) helped relieve the pain, which was becoming disabling. After much debate, she finally decided to have surgery. But afterward, the pain got worse. There was a postoperative surgical complication: fluid was leaking from the spinal cord. And further tests showed there was scar tissue pressing on the nerve in her spinal cord, so she would need even more surgery. Although the second procedure was successful, Debbie was in for a long recuperation.

During this period, Sam's father had been driving him to and from preschool every day. Then one day while I was visiting, we decided that Debbie was strong enough to go with me to pick up Sam from preschool. Sam had been told I was coming, and as soon as we pulled up, he hopped into the van, gave me a kiss on the cheek, and joined his mother in the backseat. They hugged, sorted out Sam's belongings, and talked about what he'd done in school that day. This was followed by a period of silence. As we drove along, I looked in the rearview mirror and saw Sam looking up at his mom.

"How you back today, Mommy?" he asked.

Debbie reassured him that she was feeling better and that before long she expected to be completely fine. And I had my answer. His simple question showed remarkable compassion. Whether or not things got easier for Sam, I felt reassured that he had the human capability that, to me, is so necessary. There it was—all the evidence of empathy I could have wished for. While my daughter and grandson chatted in the backseat, my eyes welled up with tears of joy and relief.

༄༅

Who taught Sam to have empathy?

I've learned that most children like Sam have the full range of emotions, but many can't express them. Looking back, I realized that evidence of Sam's empathy had been there all along. At my dad's funeral, when he was just a toddler, he insisted on sitting on my lap when I was crying. In his quick, absorbing glances, he seemed to be trying to figure out what was going on with people. I thought I'd seen empathy in the little gestures he made to help his mom or dad when they messed up; in the way he eyed my wheelchair and tried to figure out, for himself, what I could and couldn't do. He had only lacked the language to express it. Now, clearly, he had that, too, and his compassion for his mother in her pain could be put into words.

In the months and years ahead, as he talked more and more, there would be further evidence of the depth of his concerns. He found out that Debbie's mother had died before Sam was born, and with searching curiosity began quizzing Debbie about it: "What is it like not to have a mother? What would have happened if your mother lived and your father died? Are you still sad? Are you lonely without your mother?"

And he began asking me questions, too. "How did you have your accident? Are you sad that your legs can't move? Are you embarrassed about being in a wheelchair?" There was a wellspring of genuine interest and curiosity about his pop.

How lucky we are that he can wonder, and ask—that whatever challenges of learning, communicating, and socializing he may have, he also has, most fortunately, the gift of empathy.

✎✎

With very few exceptions, all of us have the ability to be empathic with the experiences of others. It's what I referred to earlier when I talked about God's fingerprint on the child's upper lip. This is the secret wisdom that God imparted to each child. Empathy could be considered part of divine inspiration. After all, that is the cornerstone of what Jesus and the Buddha preached, not to mention all of the other great thinkers and religious leaders. These injunctions—"welcome the stranger," "care for the suffering," "feed the hungry"—come not only from without but also from within. Our species could not have survived without caring for one another. We are social animals, and we live and die in community. And when we find ourselves without community and without compassion, our life expectancy is dramatically lower.

Without empathy, we might be able to function for a while, but it would come at a very steep price. We are already seeing it in today's fast-paced culture where the bottom line is more about profit and productivity and less about care and compassion. And the price we pay is that more people are taking antidepressants than ever before and more of us report having fewer intimate friends. There is ample research to show the health effects of isolation on the aging population as they become more likely to fall ill and less likely to seek medical help. But even younger people who are isolated feel its effects on their health. They are more likely to react to stressful situations with passivity—they are more at risk for hypertension and even demonstrate slower wound healing than children with social connections.

❧❧

I know there are millions of ways the power of empathy can be drummed out of us, or subverted, or discouraged. But still, throughout human history, when someone has fallen down, usually someone else has picked him up again. Why do we help each other? Because it's our way of making contact with others and ultimately with ourselves. Because it is a heartfelt longing and an evolutionary imperative. That is why we connect with another person's needs. And that is how a four-year-old boy, still struggling for words, can find a way to ask about his mother's pain.

CHAPTER 12

Was the World Only Black and White?

In my dining room, I have a number of black-and-white photographs that were taken when I was a kid. Among those family photos is a picture of me with my sister when I was four and she was nearly ten.

When Sam was about five, Debbie found her son in the dining room by himself contemplating those photographs. After a long, thoughtful pause—always the signal that Sam is working out a problem—he asked, "Was the world only black and white when you were growing up, Mommy? Or did you have colors?"

Debbie told Sam that, yes, her world came in multiple colors, even if the old photographs were just black and white. Now I don't know if it's his mind or mine that I am reading, but I don't think Sam was asking only about photography. He was asking about what his mother's world was like—both in the past and right now. That's what he wanted to figure out.

ഛൾ

Many years ago, during one of my visits to Jefferson Hospital, I witnessed an interaction between a mother and a young boy that has stayed with me.

I was in my wheelchair in a wing of the Jefferson Hospital lobby near the oncology department. The door to the cancer center swung open, and a woman in her early 30s emerged wearing a gauze turban around her head. A young boy, who looked to be no more than four years old, was holding her hand. One glance at the woman's face told the story. She had heard bad news.

As the pair approached the lobby exit, a revolving door, I saw the boy begin to hang back, visibly afraid of the spinning panes of glass.

"Mommy," he said, "I'm scared."

"I'm scared, too," she answered, "but we'll hold hands, and we'll get through together. Okay?"

Her son looked at his mother, looked at the revolving door, looked back at her, and then said, "Okay."

And together, holding hands, they went through the revolving door.

I never saw them again. I don't know what happened to that woman. But I know that in that brief moment, I witnessed loving and honest parenting at its very best.

Every time I return to that lobby in my mind's eye, my own feelings, evoked by that scene, transform. When I am with my patients, I often feel like that parent, promising them companionship and security on what can be a scary journey. And in other circumstances, I feel like that child longing for a hand to hold when my fears and anxieties seem to grow too large.

ഛൾ

After Sam studied those black-and-white photographs, he started asking questions about the people in them. Since he had never met his Aunt Sharon—shown beside me in the picture of us as children—Sam wondered who she was. What had become of her? Debbie explained that Sharon had died before Sam was born. He learned that Pop had once had a sister, that she had been married and lived far away, that she had been sick and died, all before Sam came into the world. Debbie told him as much as she thought he could absorb. Sam's thoughtful pauses, in between her answers, told Debbie that, in his five-year-old mind, he was trying to make sense of these revelations.

Sam's curiosity then, as now, was intense. There were some concepts too difficult for a five-year-old to comprehend. He knew about death, and now he knew that he'd had an Aunt Sharon who died. But he certainly couldn't understand the meaning of the words "brain tumor." Or the effect of Sharon's death on her husband, her two sons, or her brother. Even farther beyond his grasp was the story of how Sharon and Pop had grown up together, sharing life with their parents in a little house in Margate, forging the extraordinary bond of respect and love that grew deeper and stronger as they matured from childhood to adolescence and adulthood.

❧❧

Most of us censor ourselves when we talk with our children about our lives. We tell them what we think they need to hear, the aspects of our lives that we'd like them to know. We try to portray ourselves in the ways we want to be remembered. As they grow, our children get to know our values, some of our strengths, and a few weaknesses. We tell them stories of our triumphs over adversity and of our tenacity. Most children know that we love them and that they love us. But how far do we go with our honesty and openness?

As parents, many of us say we want our children to be open and honest with us, but is that really true? Are we really open to whatever they have to say? And more importantly, are we good role models for intimacy? In lectures, when I ask how many people knew their parents' values and expectations, most people in the audience raise their hands. But when I ask how many knew their parents' hearts, their dreams, their fears, not surprisingly, very few raise their hands. Then I ask, "How many of you would have *liked* to know your parents' true selves? How many of you *wanted* to know what love meant to them? How many of you *did* want to know your parents better?" Nearly all hands go up. Finally, I ask the most difficult question: "How many of your children know those things about you?"

Few hands. Sometimes none.

≪∙≫

Sam, like all our children, wants to know his parents' hearts. What comes to mind, once again, is a discussion I had some time ago with a group of high-school students about the stresses in their lives. All of these children said that their parents lived with stress and that their parents' stress contributed to their own. Most said they wanted their parents to have better lives with more joy and less work. But several children said they wanted their parents to lean on them every now and then. As I explored this further, I learned that not only did these children want to care for their parents but they also wanted to hear their stories when they were vulnerable or sad. They longed for that kind of intimacy.

Children like Sam need us as role models. Not to model perfect strength, moral rectitude, or unwavering purpose.

Sure, to very small children, all that matters is how well they are cared for. But as they age, they need something more. Older children might still need our care, but they also need to explore the world in their own ways. They need to know that it's normal to struggle sometimes with ambivalence, insecurity, low self-esteem, impulsivity, and envy. If they don't know their parents feel this way from time to time, how will they feel about themselves when they have their own struggles? There's the risk that what is natural and human will be labeled pathology. Normal grief becomes depression and gets medicated. Normal wakefulness becomes insomnia and gets medicated. Normal agitation becomes attention deficit disorder.

If we, as adults, can't talk about our own shame, insecurity, or vulnerability, our children will feel they can't either. The message becomes: "There's something wrong with you that will be treated and fixed or that you will outgrow." But that's not what our children need. Like Sam, they want to know what our world is really like. They need to hear us say, "I lived with that, too. I still do. You're not alone in feeling the way you do. It's okay. I know you may be scared sometimes. So am I. But we'll hold hands and somehow get through."

∽⁀⁀

When my children were in high school and they wanted to know about drugs, I was honest with them about my history. When I was growing up, none of the kids I knew in high school had anything to do with drugs. I didn't smoke pot until my sophomore year in college, which was in 1965, when it seemed like suddenly everyone was doing it. Despite current wisdom that says not to, I told my daughters which drugs I experimented with and which ones I didn't touch. I also told them which ones I was afraid of—particularly cocaine and hallucinogens. I said some experiences had made me feel good. Others, terrible. I described some of the things I had seen happen to my friends while doing drugs, and that most of those friends just seemed to outgrow it but some didn't. I also told them about how one of my friends died of an overdose.

Then I said that *their* experimenting with drugs scared me and explained why. Partly because I was their father. Partly because their brains were four years younger than mine had been when I first tried marijuana. Partly because the drugs widely available today are so much more powerful than when I was young. I also told them that if they did try drugs, I hoped they would feel safe enough to talk to me about it before, during, or after.

The evening before an important lecture, I received a call from one of my daughters. I was in my hotel room preparing my talk when the phone rang. I answered and heard a familiar voice.

"Dad," my daughter said, "there's a party tonight and I think I'm going to try mescaline. What do you think?"

I told her, "The idea of taking hallucinogens has always scared me. I've been afraid of losing that much control of my mind, and as a psychologist, I have seen too many people who were too injured by these drugs. Not only that, the idea of *you* taking them really scares me! But I know you're going to do what you're going to do because that's who you are. But if things go bad, you call me any time today, tonight, or tomorrow. Don't hesitate for a second. I'm here to help you."

Then we said goodbye. That night, as she was out partying, I was up worrying. She didn't call. In the morning, I was exhausted, but I got through my lecture, and I talked to her later. She was fine; in fact, she was in better shape than I was.

Did it make a difference, to her, that her father could talk to her about his own experience? Did it make a difference, to me, that she could tell me what she was going to do and, afterward, what it had been like for her? I don't know. What I do know is that we held hands and got through that door together.

✧✦

As I write, three years have passed since Sam asked his mother about those black-and-white photographs in my dining room. I'm a little sad because Sam is growing so fast. But I'm also excited because he's just at the age where I can begin to ask *him* the questions.

As for Sam, his curiosity seems to grow stronger every day. Behind so many of his questions, I hear the kinds of things I too have always wondered about. His eyes are opening wider and, every day, in so many ways, I can see him beginning to touch on bigger questions and bigger ideas, like "Who am I?" and "How am I different from my parents?" And "If I am different, does that mean I'm alone?"

When he's ready, that last question is one I can answer. "Yes, my sweet grandson, ultimately you are alone, in the sense that no one else can really understand what it's like to be Sam."

But I know Sam pretty well and I know a bit about humans, so I would imagine Sam's final question would be: "Well, can we be *different* and still be together?"

Yes, Sam, once we understand that we are alone and once we stop trying to change it, then we can all be alone together. Then we will have lots of hands to hold the next time we face one of life's revolving doors.

CHAPTER 13

Where Bad Dreams Go

What kid wouldn't be fascinated by the mysterious circumstances surrounding the Bermuda Triangle? Within the triangular area of the Atlantic Ocean between Bermuda, Puerto Rico, and the tip of Florida, scores of ships and planes are said to have disappeared literally without a trace. Could the Bermuda Triangle be a place where travelers and their vessels entered some kind of time warp that sped them into the past or future? Or perhaps the area is frequented by UFOs and samples of earthlings are seized by extraterrestrials for their diabolical experiments. Whatever the terrors that lurk in this zone, it's a great source of wonder and speculation, especially for someone who is eight years old.

Sam has a pretty good understanding of the shape and size of the world, particularly its seas and oceans, because his father is an avid sailor. Sam has just started to learn to sail, and when he's a little older, he will begin taking lessons at the sailing camp where Pat teaches during the summer. In the meantime, they talk about places to travel. Sam has a globe of the world, and when he has a question about where things are located or where someone is headed, Pat helps him find that spot on the globe. It was one of these discussions that took them to the Bermuda Triangle.

After tracing the outlines of that triangular sea where so many sailors, pilots, and passengers met their mysterious fates, Sam sank into a moment of reflection. Then he looked up at his dad.

"The Bermuda Triangle," said Sam. "Is that where bad dreams go?"

⋘⋙

According to his mom, Sam doesn't have terrible nightmares. Instead, when he wakens in the night and needs some consoling, it's over issues that Debbie describes as "more like the anxieties of a 40-year-old man." Sam worries about what may happen in school the next day, whether he will be prepared, how he will meet potential challenges. His "bad dreams" are distressing but not terrifying. He's not pursued by demons and monsters. It's more like he just frets and worries about being prepared, being safe, or being ready for what the next day will bring. Sam, like most of his genetic donors, has a worrying brain. Even at his tender age, he has lots of experience with bad dreams. They may be painful for part of the night—but after that? Well, they vanish when he wakes up. Perhaps, as he suggests, they go to the Bermuda Triangle, where he doesn't have to tussle with them anymore.

What Sam calls bad dreams, I'm more likely to call painful emotions. However we label them, we can always count on having them, whether they come to us during the day or keep us tossing and turning at night. Sometimes these bad dreams loom in the background without our being fully aware of them—a sense of foreboding, the background noise of anxiety, or a belief that we are just not good enough. And our first instinct is to do whatever we can to make that unease go away.

Sylvia Boorstein, a Buddhist teacher and Jewish theologian, titled one of her books *Don't Just Do Something, Sit There*. As a therapist, that's what I tell people. When you're in doubt, do nothing. And then, when you're confident, still do nothing. Just sit there. (I figure if I keep my mouth shut, I'm much less likely to put my foot in it!)

When I offer this advice, some people look puzzled because it's counterintuitive. But Boorstein is right. If we can just have the dream or the fear or the disease and *do nothing*—just let it be a part of our lives—it's less likely to stay.

It's not pain that causes us problems, it's the fact that we don't think we can tolerate our pain. Young as he is, Sam is beginning to learn that bad feelings sometimes really are bad, but eventually they are all replaced by other feelings. Sam still feels great anxiety about his anxiety, though he and his mother (and the therapy he has been in) have helped him develop some pretty good coping mechanisms. But my wish for Sam is that he also learns that most bad dreams are temporary visitors: they leave pretty soon if we don't see them as adversaries that need to be wrestled with.

❧❧

Of course, some bad dreams bring us valuable information. Often they tell us about emotions that have been buried in our psyches.

Some time after 9/11, a friend brought her eight-year-old son, Andy, to talk to me about the fear that was waking him up each night. I usually don't see children that young, let alone children of friends, but I thought I might be able to offer her some guidance if we met over milk and cookies. Andy had just learned about the planes crashing into the

World Trade Center and the people who were killed. The images were so shocking that Andy stayed awake at night, scared that planes would fly into his house at any moment and kill his family. His mother couldn't figure out what to do. Should she stay by his bedside when he woke up? Leave him by himself to deal with it? Or let him get up and go outside to see that everything was fine? Nothing she had tried so far had helped make his anxiety go away.

When I talked to Andy, I told him that he was at an age where children first learn about life and death and that one day their parents will die. Some kids seem to learn this and move on. But for other kids, it stays with them. Andy was one of those kids. I had been, too. So I told him about the boogeyman who used to hide under my bed when I was about his age. I was terrified of that boogeyman, and the only way I could keep him away was to lie absolutely still. If I so much as moved my eyes, he would know I was lying in the bed right on top of him and he would come and kill me and my family. Night after night, I lay there motionless, dreading what might happen.

Like any curious boy, Andy wanted to know what became of the boogeyman. "Is he still under there?" he asked me.

"I've got to be honest," I said. "The boogeyman is still under there, but after all these years, he's old, and he's been there for so long I know he can't hurt me anymore. He can keep me up at night, but he can't hurt me because he's an old guy like me."

That seemed to make Andy feel better. After all, if an old guy like me had been living with his boogeyman all those years—and survived—maybe Andy would be okay, too. He, too, would make it through those nights when he was alone with his fears.

I hate to say this, but I believe Sam will always have his anxiety, just like his pop. After all, he's got the genetics and he's got this tender heart that puts people at risk for anxiety. But I hope that Sam realizes that his anxiety is simply a part of his brain and that it's not the voice of truth. I compare my anxiety to beach glass. It starts off jagged and dangerous, but over time it becomes soft around the edges, even beautiful in its own way. I hope deeply that Sam's anxiety turns to beach glass. I wish that for all of us.

CHAPTER 14

Great Expectations

Suppose you were packing for a long weekend at what we'll call Hazy Resorts, a luxury retreat in the Caribbean. Naturally, you would bring along all the necessities for your personal comfort. Assuming you have average needs, you'd need a couple of changes of underwear and the requisite items for grooming and personal hygiene—a toothbrush, comb, and deodorant. Some casual clothes to wear during the day, a few dressier clothes for the evening, a couple of pairs of shoes, a bathing suit—oh, and pajamas, if you wear them. All set? Anything you've forgotten?

It's a comfortable flight and an uneventful ride from the airport. You arrive at the resort, where you're greeted warmly by your host. Then, just before you're shown to your room, the host takes you into a large room where other new arrivals, just like you, are waiting for their rooms. And all of them, just like you, have their suitcases and traveling bags.

The host remains polite, but he asks everyone to open their bags and hand over their shoes. Surprised? I'll bet. But when you look around, unbelievable as it may seem, none of the other guests seems even slightly put out!

It gets worse. After the host has collected the shoes, he puts them into a single bin and says they will be for everyone. Any time you want shoes, just come to this bin, take the pair you want, and then put them back when you're through.

Then things get really bizarre. Next, the host goes around and collects all the shirts and pants. They go into a second bin. Again, your fellow guests seem comfortable with the requests. And so it goes. Socks are put into a great big plastic bag. Hats are collected on a shelf at the far end of the room. All the jackets are assembled in one common closet, sweaters in another. Finally, you're left with only your pajamas and your personal toiletry items. Those items, the host tells you cheerily, you can keep.

❧❧

Welcome to Sam's first day in second grade. Here's how it works at Sam's school. A few weeks before classes begin, teachers send out notices to all the parents of second graders, welcoming the new students and providing parents some details about the upcoming year. Included is a list of items that students should plan to bring to school on their first day. In addition to pencils, erasers, and colored markers, they'll also need a bottle of hand sanitizer, several boxes of tissues, and a number of other personal items.

Debbie and Sam review the list and pack carefully. Sam counts out the pencils, erasers, and markers, and puts them in his pack where he can easily find them. Debbie shows him the side pocket where she places the hand sanitizer. Sam picks out his favorite packages of nose blowers (his term for tissues) and adds them to the private cache. All with mounting anticipation, along with a substantial dose of anxiety. For Sam, there are special difficulties in situations such as these. During the previous three weeks, as summer vacation was drawing to a close, Sam spent nearly all his time at home with his mother. "Will I be okay without you?" he wondered aloud as he looked ahead to the start of school. Debbie discussed it with him. They worked out a plan for the first day. Debbie suggested that she could come to school just before lunch to bring in his Lactaid (a dietary pill that Sam needs to counteract the effect of lactose intolerance). When she did, she and Sam would have a few moments alone when he could tell her privately how things were going.

That plan helped Sam get ready.

Debbie also gave Sam a careful preview of the day, helping him visualize what would happen at school. He had already met his teacher, Mrs. Craig, and he liked her. Debbie assured Sam that Mrs. Craig would meet him at the classroom door along with the other children and help him find his desk. Debbie predicted that Mrs. Craig would give Sam a detailed introduction to the day's activities along with an overview of what he could expect to happen in the first week.

By the time the bus arrived on that first day, Sam was well prepped. He waved goodbye to his mom and departed from home without a backward glance.

During the morning, Debbie worried. For her own sake, as well as Sam's, she was glad to have prearranged an excuse to meet him before lunchtime. Arriving at school at the designated time, she spoke a few words with Mrs. Craig, who indicated that everything seemed to be going well. As she'd hoped, Debbie then had a few moments to confer with Sam when she was giving him his medicine.

That was when he broke the bad news to her. That morning, something terrible had happened.

ᨀᨁᨂ

We all have a vision of the way the world should work, and we become more or less attached to that vision. Then along come some surprises, and whether those surprises are good or bad, because we're strongly attached to that image of "the way things should be," we tend to react negatively. When children are on the autism spectrum, they become more attached than most to the "pictures" they have inside their heads. They have a great need for order. More order, more security. Less order, more anxiety. But though these attachments may seem excessive or exaggerated, they are really no different from our own. Research shows that the more anxiety goes up, the more we tend to clutch on to our belief systems. The more internally secure we feel, the more flexible we are.

Our children come into this world with their own temperament and genetic loading. And we are learning more about parental influence or lack thereof. But we do know this—that for the child's psyche to flourish, he or she must have a healthy attachment during the early years. Our children need a parent figure who is predictable and available. Ideally a parent who can go beyond meeting a child's biological needs and spend time with him or her in a relaxed, loving, and spacious way. This way the child can learn directly and through role modeling that the world is a safe and loving place.

On the other hand, children raised by extremely anxious parents who may be overprotective or overbearing will absorb that anxiety. The same goes for children who are raised by parents who are uninvolved. In both cases, these children worry more about the environment than about themselves. They "learn" early on that their welfare depends on a stable environment. So naturally, these children (and later adults) work very hard to make sure the environment is "just so" in order to feel stable and secure.

And the more anxiety that child feels, the more he or she needs the environment to be predictable.

Sam had an image of the way the world was supposed to look on his first day of second grade. But it wasn't that way, and boy, did he suffer. And it all began with the loss of what he thought was his personal property.

৵৵

Here's what went wrong.

As Sam and his mom loaded up his backpack for school, he was heartened by the expectation that all these carefully picked personal items would be right where he put them. At any time during the school day, he assumed, he could reach into his pack and find his pencils and erasers, colored markers, hand washer, and nose blowers. But there was something Debbie hadn't anticipated and Sam could never have imagined. Eighty percent of the items he brought to school were meant to be shared by everyone in the class!

"We'll put all the erasers here," said Mrs. Craig, holding up a plastic bin. "Any time you need to use an eraser, just take one of these, and return it when you're done."

All around Sam, the other students carried their erasers forward to the plastic bin and dropped them in, just as Mrs. Craig had requested. Blindsided by this procedure, helpless to resist, Sam, I'm sure, wondered how things could have gone so wrong. But there was little he could do except follow the teacher's instructions.

The nightmare continued. Mrs. Craig collected the markers. Then the pencils. Soon, nearly all the items in Sam's backpack were lost among his fellow students' confiscated belongings where he would never find them again.

By the time Debbie arrived at Sam's school, the morning's damage was done. All the meticulous care that had gone into Sam and Debbie's joint preparations had been undone in minutes by Mrs. Craig. He didn't care about his property being taken away, he cared that his sense of order was destroyed. And making matters worse, all of the other children seemed to understand what was happening and Sam didn't. So he felt very alone and embarrassed by his confusion.

❧❧

Is it easier for us, as adults, to let go of our expectations? To lose the unrealistic (and unrealized) pictures that are in our minds? Can we walk into the next classroom without any attachments or preconceived notions?

I think we've all been to a version of Hazy Resorts. A place where we imagined that everything would be fine, everything would be perfect. And then . . .

I think of a friend who grew up in a troubled family. Her mother was incapable of selfless love. Rejected by her own parents, my friend was ultimately raised by a member of her extended family. But like most children raised in dysfunctional families, she had a picture of what a "real" family would be like. Because of her background, she felt different and very much alone. So she thought if she had the family she'd pictured, she would no longer be unhappy.

My friend got married and thought she would live out that picture. And for a while, she did. She had beautiful, healthy children, and they did everything healthy families are supposed to do. But over time she realized her husband wasn't the loving man she thought he was, and she was still unhappy. So despite coming close, this family didn't fit the one in her head. Again, she was heartbroken and disappointed.

These feelings continued for ten years, until her daughter got married. My friend thought that now, perhaps, her daughter at least would experience that beautiful picture of family life, and that she could be the loving grandmother. But that picture didn't work out either, and again she was heartbroken. What was it that caused this lifetime of disappointment? The facts of her life, or her own expectations?

Everything in our mind and body calls for us to attach to those images of what *should be*. Once we create those expectations, we tell ourselves, *That's where I'll find security.* And it works—briefly. When we attach, we feel secure. But then the insecurity creeps back in again. If Mrs. Craig doesn't take our things away, someone else—or something else—will. I certainly had a picture of my life 30 years ago before I became quadriplegic, but then everything changed. Over time, I developed a new picture of my life—but then my wife left. And so, throughout my life, whatever pictures I have clutched have been pulled from my grasp.

By the end of Sam's first day of second grade, he had mostly recovered from his confusion and shame. He had begun the process of understanding that expectations can go unfulfilled, order can be shattered, and in the wake of that, we can feel anxiety and insecurity. Those are facts. But the precious lesson that Sam started to learn at the age of eight is the same one that I started to learn 30 years ago. Surprises happen, we suffer, and then we recover. All we have to do is stop grasping for that image in our heads and allow our hearts to heal as they always do. In the process, we can live the lives we already have instead of waiting for the lives we wish for.

CHAPTER 15

A Bus for Sam's Pop

I am no ordinary Phillies fan. I am a Phillies fan with special needs, which means there are major logistics that have to be addressed before the first pitch. Loyal to my team, I go to a number of home games every summer. By now, I'm pretty good at getting around Citizens Bank Park. But if I went to another ballpark, I'd be starting over as far as logistics are concerned. I'd have to figure it out all over again.

What I find is that the first time I'm in any new territory—a bookstore, a lecture hall, an airport, a restaurant, a hotel—I tend to be hypervigilant. Glancing at a doorway, I wonder, *Can I get through that?* Looking at a desk or counter, I'm instinctively figuring out if my legs can get under. If I'm not watching out for myself and making those on-the-spot decisions, I could get stuck at any time. Hence the hypervigilance.

Debbie maintains this kind of vigilance, too. She can often anticipate tactical issues and deal with them before they become a problem. And recently, I've come to realize that Sam, over the past few years, has been developing a similar kind of awareness. He is keenly aware of his surroundings, and like his mother, Sam is not just paying attention for his own sake. Certainly, he's making mental calculations that help ensure his own safety and security. But he's also working out larger problems.

Here's what I mean: at the most basic level, a kid quickly figures out how high the steps are; which doors he can open and which ones he can't; how far he has to stand from a sprinkler to avoid getting wet; and, if he's a boy, where to aim when he pees (Sam had to do a bit of work on that one). But those are the basics. By the age of six, Sam, with his unusual empathy for others and his newly developed strategic skills, was beginning to figure things out for others.

From the outset, he's never shown any anxiety—and certainly no shame—about his pop being in a wheelchair. On the contrary, grandpop-in-a-wheelchair was his first experience with grandpops. I think he just assumed we all come this way. The wheelchair was something to climb on and run around, but it didn't signify to Sam what it does to others—that its occupant was disabled or handicapped or, for that matter, inconvenienced in any way. At the same time, Sam did see the engineering and logistical challenges that can occur when someone is constantly seated in a heavy motorized chair that won't go up stairs.

So, the first time Sam saw a bus that had a wheelchair lift, he recognized an excellent solution to a problem that had apparently been puzzling him for quite a while. At age five, Sam had started taking the bus to school. He knew how to climb up the short, steep stairs onto the yellow school bus, walk along the narrow aisle, and take his seat. But in the back of his mind, all along, he must have been trying to figure out how Pop could accomplish the same mission. Though he'd never discussed it aloud, this must have been a nagging concern. If grandpops could not get on a school bus, how could they go to school?

Then he saw a public handicap-accessible bus. It had a wheelchair lift! Something clicked. Problem solved. He turned to his mom and asked, "Is that wheelchair bus so that the children can bring their grandpops to school?"

Debbie had to admit that the primary purpose of a handicap-accessible bus was not to bring grandpops to school. But she also let Sam know it was an excellent idea. And, certainly, it solved a problem that had been puzzling him: How can we get Pop to do as many things as possible?

❧❦

Since then, Sam's mind has gone to work on quite a number of other logistical challenges, and we never know where the next innovative idea will come from. Consider, for instance, this wheelchair challenge: I can cruise anywhere along the boardwalk that runs from Atlantic City south along the outer beach. The boardwalk is wide enough to accommodate several lanes of walkers, bike riders, and the occasional wheelchair, and the planks are so smooth that I can pick up some speed. Access is good from the side streets, and there are, in some places, concrete ramps and pull-outs where I can get a great view of the beach. So far, so good. But I can't go down to the beach with Sam! The ramps that go over the dunes lead straight into soft sand, and if I drove onto it, my chair would immediately sink down to its hubcaps (and, no doubt, the sand would destroy the motor).

Sam figured out a solution. All we had to do, he explained, was build a platform that someone could pull up to the end of the concrete ramp that leads onto the beach. The platform would cover the sand. Pop could drive his wheelchair onto the platform, then someone could drag the platform over the sand. That way, Pop could go anywhere on the beach.

It's an elegant solution (as soon as we can hire the tractor or 12-horse team that will drag the platform along the beach). But what impresses me most is not the engineering marvel that Sam has developed, but the way he's done this brainwork, not for himself but for his pop. I can see his problem-solving left brain in high gear and at the same time his loving, compassionate right brain motivating the process. It all makes me marvel and wonder what's next.

≪≫

There are already plentiful signs that Sam can use this ingenuity to help meet his own challenges.

As I write, Sam has been working on the problem of how to sleep by himself. Apart from that first trip to the shore with Mr. Pete, and a few times in the hospital by himself, Sam has slept with his mom and dad almost every night. It began when he was an infant. As a baby, he was very quiet—never stirring in his sleep, never crying out. (In hindsight, we know these were probably early signs of his autism.) Concerned that they wouldn't know if Sam was in distress, Debbie and Pat got in the habit of bringing Sam into their bed as a safety measure. Later on, Sam began waking up frequently during the night, and often he was in distress. Now, when he wakes up, he is better able to explain what's happening to him, which helps a bit. Nevertheless, he still feels he needs the immediate comfort of his mother or father in the middle of the night, to know they will be there to help allay the anxiety he's feeling at that moment. So far, it seems to be the only way he can deal with his fear and get back to sleep.

But now he's eight years old and going to school, and he knows that other kids don't sleep with their parents. He doesn't want to, either. He's ready to move on. But he wonders what will happen when he wakes in the night and can't have quick access to his parents. He'll be alone with his anxieties. How will he deal with fear by himself? Like most people with anxiety, Sam is afraid of his fear.

In lengthy discussions with Debbie and Pat, he has started to solve this logistical problem. Sam proposes to start sleeping on an air mattress on the floor next to his mother's side of the bed, since she's the one he usually turns to when he wakes up in the night. After a while, he'll move the mattress around to his dad's side and sleep there. Finally, he'll take it to his own room and try sleeping by himself.

What Sam has proposed, in his own creative way, would be roundly applauded by the psychotherapist Joseph Wolpe, who in the 1950s developed a treatment program for anxiety that came to be called systematic desensitization. Wolpe's idea was to gradually expose patients to what they feared and then help them practice relaxation techniques to cope with the fear. And to this day, variations on that treatment are the gold standard for a variety of anxiety disorders. Sam is perfectly aware of what he fears—sleeping by himself. And his clever scheme of "graduating" to an air mattress, then moving the air mattress farther and farther away, is his own way of gradually building his endurance to the point where he can get through every night on his own.

I'm impressed but not surprised. To Sam, the problem that needs to be solved just happens to be what goes on inside his head. Already he seems to have a remarkable ability to think about his own thoughts and—when those thoughts present a problem—look for a practical resolution.

I suspect that this transition, for Sam, is going to be as difficult as many of the other steps he has taken in his young life. For one thing, I'm quite sure his nighttime anxieties will not go away completely. Given his personality and his genetics, it's likely that his anxiety will recur throughout his life. Sometimes fears can be dealt with when they are anticipated. Whether we know it or not, we all strategize to avoid what will potentially cause fear. But we also know that fears will visit us when we are *not* expecting them and in ways that we can't strategize our way out of.

My great wish for Sam is that, over time, he'll learn that his fear will come and go and will not hurt him. Sam's brilliant plan will give him freedom from his parents' room. But if he can learn, one day, not to be afraid of his own anxieties, his sense of freedom will become something that lives inside of him, accessible whenever he needs it.

CHAPTER 16

I Am More Kind

Now that Sam is eight years old, we can sit down together and have a regular discussion. Of course, he has a limited tolerance for many of the topics that grownups find interesting. But he can be remarkably forthcoming about his own experiences, and already he seems to know some important things about himself and his personal qualities.

During one conversation, we talked about some of the experiences he'd had when he was younger. The subject of autism came up. Sam said he'd had autism when he was younger but he didn't have it anymore "except sometimes." Still, he realized that because of his autism he hadn't started talking as soon as the other kids and that was the reason why he had started school a year later than they did. So autism explained why he was a year older than most kids in his class. But when I asked him to describe the "sometimes" when he still has autism, he was stumped. It seemed mostly a thing of the past.

So I turned the conversation to things that I thought he might remember about the learning process. When he first began to express himself, he used sign language. At the age of eight, he still recalled some of the hand gestures that spelled out his name, but he had forgotten how to say "I love you" in sign language. Other memories, however, were still vivid:

"I used to have a friend named Drew, and we had a cat named Paco," he recalled. "We had a babysitter named Adida, and that's pretty much it." Then he concluded, "We used to ride a tractor down a very steep hill. We used to go to a lake that had a playground that I loved. Mostly the swing. It is still my favorite."

So, all conscious memory of his past struggles had been left behind. What he remembered were the kinds of things any kid would remember—a friend, a pet, a babysitter, a favorite playground. Still, I wondered how he felt about himself right now.

"Sam, do you feel you are the same as the other kids?" I asked. "Or different?"

He thought for a moment. "Different," he said.

What do you think makes you different from the other kids?"

"I am more kind."

That observation of Sam's came back to me a couple of weeks later when he was at my house. Sam and I decided we would play some basketball. He threw the ball, aiming for the hoop while I positioned myself underneath, trying to catch the ball in my lap. Sometimes I caught the ball, sometimes I didn't, but I noticed that whether I did or not, Sam always had a compliment for me—"Great catch, Pop!" or "Good try!"

And I thought, you know, Sam's right about himself. He's incredibly kind.

❧❧

Of course, not everyone is that kind. And I feel protective of the tender heart that shows so much kindness. He already sees how his "being nice" makes him different from the other kids. He's not bragging. It's not a special virtue. It's just the way he is.

But I wonder, after 10 or 20 years have passed, will his heart still be so open? Will the world around him change in response to that kindness, or will the world change *him?* A little of each, I suspect.

A parent's instinct would be to warn Sam about the world that he's going to be facing. (Isn't that what protective parents are supposed to do—inform their children about the way things *really* work?) That parent might tell him that he will be constantly measured against his peers. He'll have to compete with them for everything—a place in school, a job, status in the community, and a position in society.

Perhaps a nice kid like Sam should be warned about people who may not care about his feelings. Should he be told that people might make fun of him or take advantage of him because of his kindness? After all, there are people who simply don't care who gets hurt. And he'll have to find out—either from his parents or from someone else—that though we love him and want the best for him, we won't always be there to protect him. And if, through all that, he persists with his kindness, will he find anyone who appreciates it?

❧❧

Although we can't predict Sam's future, I have some insight because I was also a child with a tender heart. I remember being in my father's Army-Navy store with my mother when a customer came in to buy a flannel shirt. Like most of the customers, he was a day laborer with dirty hands and tired eyes. When he saw the price of the shirt, he said he couldn't afford it because he wasn't getting very much work these days and asked if he could get a discount. Instead, my mother showed him a very nice shirt that was less expensive but not quite as warm. I remember feeling so sad for him and angry that my mother didn't help him. She told me that many people say things like that just to get a discount and that I shouldn't be so naïve. I still believed him, and I still felt sad.

That story could have been repeated dozens of times throughout my childhood. And each time, my response earned me a lot of warnings. I recall my mother and even my extended family telling me that I was naïve for trusting people, that the world was tough, and that people wouldn't treat me the way I treated them. I was told I was "too sensitive" and would be hurt.

In a way, these messages are understandable. All of my aunts and uncles were children of people who had lived under unspeakable conditions in Russia and were victims of hatred every day of their lives. So when they raised their children, no doubt they felt a strong parental responsibility to teach them about "the world as it really is." This is the message many tenderhearted children get from well-intentioned parents trying to protect them from future pain. Of course the warnings never work. And the children only feel more "different" because even their parents don't understand them.

∽♾∾

When the antidepressant Prozac first hit the market, it seemed like a miracle drug. Not only was it having a dramatic impact on people with depression, it also appeared to help with eating disorders of all kinds, not to mention a variety of other psychological problems. Shortly after its introduction,

I had the opportunity to interview Peter Kramer, M.D., author of *Listening to Prozac,* and ask him why this drug was having an impact on so many diverse problems. He thought for a minute and then replied, "Everybody is born with a different amount of Teflon on their nerve endings. It seems that Prozac simply adds another layer of Teflon."

I thought that was a wonderful analogy. Almost immediately, I thought of people I have treated over the years—people with very little Teflon who were reactive to almost everything in their environment. These people were easily wounded and were at risk for depression and anxiety disorders.

∞⟨⟩∞

Some time ago, I treated a young girl who seemed to have almost no Teflon. Sixteen-year-old Annette had one of the most tender hearts of anyone I'd ever met. She was sent to me because of severe depression. Her parents noticed that she had been spending more time in her room and stopped socializing with her friends.

When I first saw her, Annette was wearing a hoodie that she'd pulled over her head. Though it was a warm spring day, her face was so covered up that I could hardly see her. From beneath the edge of the hood her dark eyes revealed the sadness she felt in her heart.

In a voice barely above a whisper, she told me about a girl in her school who had cerebral palsy and how the kids were making fun of her. Too shy to intervene, Annette said she could feel this little girl's pain. She went on to describe her feelings for many others, too—the girl who was the most unpopular in the class and the boy who got hollered at by the teacher because he didn't get his homework done on time. And when she learned about the children starving in Africa, she began to feel guilty about having all the comforts she had. Yes, Annette was depressed, and many people would say her depression explained her reaction to all of the other children. But that's far from the whole story. She was also a child with a tender heart that couldn't handle all of the pain she saw around her.

When Annette came in, she said she felt so very alone in this world because no one understood her. She sometimes felt she was the only person who cared so deeply about other people's suffering. So we talked about tender hearts and how many people have them. I told her about Sam and me and how many people like us care deeply about the suffering in the world. But at this moment, it seemed as if Annette was experiencing that kind of suffering. It was as though she absorbed people's pain without a filter.

There's a concept in Chinese medicine called a heart protector. This is the body's natural way of protecting a tender heart. I told her that her heart protector might not be doing its job. Because if it had been, she would be able to feel not only compassion for those who suffer but also great joy for all of the beauty in the world.

Annette seemed to understand this. She wanted to know how to get more protection for her heart. I told her that I didn't know much about Chinese medicine so she should consult a doctor trained in it. I told her that I did know a lot about psychotherapy—and that good therapy, and sometimes medication, could help her develop some of what she needed to protect her heart.

In her case, that combination worked well. It helped her get through high school and find a wonderful college. When I saw her later, she told me enthusiastically about her involvement in the college's anti-poverty campaign. I was not surprised.

⨂⨂

Like Annette's, my tender heart caused me to have a low-grade depression for much of my childhood. But it also allowed me to make a lot of friends and keep them, to care deeply about all living beings, and to love easily. When I think back on my conversations with Annette, I sometimes wonder what I could have said to her parents that would help them understand their child. I know it wasn't easy for my parents to get a sense of what was going on with me. Annette's parents faced a similar challenge.

Well, my advice would have been something like this: First, be thankful that you have a kind, sensitive child. Second, please don't try to talk her out of her emotions. If you do, she will feel as though she is doing something wrong. These sweet children need to find an outlet to channel their care.

With Annette, I could detect an immediate gleam of interest when we started talking about things she could do to help others. This is so true of kids like these. When they start to balance their care for others with caring for themselves, it enables them to have more fun in their lives. My daughter Ali blossomed when she began doing volunteer work at a kennel; her compassion for homeless animals had, at last, found a form of expression. Other kids like her are thrilled when they can visit a retirement home, raise money for a good cause, or bring food or even just company to a homebound neighbor. When a child needs to express care for people and the world, what more can a parent wish for?

❦

Sure, Sam will need help preparing for the world he is going to face. The world is competitive, and one must learn and achieve in order to develop. But I will let his parents and teachers take care of that. I want to do what I can to make sure that when Sam is an adult, he can look in the mirror and see a man who still values kindness.

CHAPTER 17

My Death

One evening I was on the phone talking to a friend when I was overcome by a dizzy spell. I was familiar with these spells, but previously they had always occurred in the morning when the cause was postural hypotension, a condition in which blood pressure falls rapidly when someone sits up suddenly. The morning fall in blood pressure, accompanied by dizziness, would be caused by the elevation from a prone position to a seated position when my nurse lifted me to give me my bath or put me in my wheelchair. But this wasn't the morning; it was the evening. And I knew something was wrong.

I was so dizzy and disoriented that I couldn't even operate the control stick on my wheelchair, and my nurse had to help steer me back to the bedroom. The next day, I called my doctor, who sent me to a cardiologist. What concerned him was my heartbeat. It had always been slow—a typical symptom of spinal-cord injury—but now it was slower than ever. The cardiologist put me in a Holter monitor that tracked my heartbeat for the next 48 hours.

The moment the doctor saw the results, he called me from his office. He wanted me to call an ambulance immediately. "You need a pacemaker right away," he told me. The monitor had shown that my heart rate was dangerously slow. The doctor didn't know why. But he knew that something had to be done quickly. The monitor had revealed that when I slept, my heart sometimes stopped beating for as long as four seconds.

Having the pacemaker installed proved to be a straightforward procedure. I was in and out of the hospital in one day. After that, though, I started to have wild fluctuations in my blood pressure. We knew that was caused by some dysfunction in my autonomic nervous system, which controls parts of the body that function "automatically," like the heart, blood vessels, and glands. The autonomic system is typically impaired by quadriplegia—I knew that. But this was a symptom that couldn't be explained. None of the doctors could figure out why blood-pressure fluctuations would follow the installation of a pacemaker.

In the days that followed, my blood pressure skyrocketed and plummeted whenever there was the slightest stimulation. The changes were so dramatic that, when I called the ER and quoted the numbers over the phone, the physician claimed it was impossible. No one, he said, could survive that kind of rapid fluctuation of blood pressure. There must be something wrong with the readings on my blood-pressure machine.

In fact, there was nothing wrong with the machine. But there was definitely something wrong with my body. The dizzy spells and the rapid fluctuations in blood pressure continued.

The autonomic nervous system is complicated. Though it controls so many parts of the body, few doctors specialize in its function. The person who implanted my pacemaker was an electrophysiologist, a cardiologist who specialized in electrical impulses. He couldn't explain what was happening. Technically, rehabilitation doctors also know a lot about the effects of spinal-cord injury on the autonomic system but none specialize. I learned that, technically, autonomic-system study comes under the umbrella of neurology, but again almost no one specializes. So I felt alone in this process. In medicine, as in other professions where people become highly specialized, there's a phenomenon known as "turfing off." Is that what was happening to me? Was everyone "turfing me off"?

After I talked to several doctors and was given a variety of tests and diagnoses, I finally found a specialist at the Mayo Clinic who was kind enough to exchange e-mails with me and offer some guidance. I also consulted with the Kennedy Krieger Institute, a rehabilitation facility associated with Johns Hopkins School of Medicine. I learned a few more things about autonomic-system functioning, but no one knew exactly what was wrong or what to do.

In my own mind, the most honest explanation was summed up by two of the doctors I consulted, who told me that, in all likelihood, my body was just wearing out. Already I had lived much longer than most quadriplegics. Now we were entering new territory, where no medical practitioner could predict what would happen next. After all these years, my heart wasn't broken, but it was tired.

During these days of diagnostics and consultation, I went from feeling scared and alone to just feeling sad that my precious life felt like it was slipping away. Debbie and Pat, of course, knew all that was going on with me, and they were pretty worried. While I don't think they'd discussed any of the details with Sam—nor had I—I am sure his parents told him that Pop was sick. And, knowing Sam, he could see how worried they were. In turn, he worried.

A year after my pacemaker had been implanted, my heart rate steadied. But my blood pressure continued to vary

121

wildly and unpredictably. Repeatedly, I had moments when I would suddenly get dizzy almost to the point of blacking out. I couldn't trust myself to drive. I felt tremendous fatigue most of the time. My energy would drop so precipitously that, at times, I had to fight for the strength to do the simplest thing, like brushing my teeth in the morning. Sometimes, my chest muscles would become so fatigued that I couldn't speak above a whisper.

But in a strange way, while all of this was going on, I felt more alive. I said to someone that I could sometimes feel my death kissing me on one cheek. And when I did, I could feel my life kissing me on the other. As I saw the light of my life begin to flicker, it felt like all colors were more vivid, my relationships more tender, my gratitude more accessible, and my heart more open.

In the midst of all this, Debbie, Pat, Sam, and I got together for a summer weekend in Atlantic City. We were out at the local ice-cream stand. Debbie and Pat were off to one side having some kind of discussion when Sam approached me with a visible look of discomfort. As he sidled up to my wheelchair, his eyes were downcast and he just didn't look like the usual Sam.

"Pop," he said, fumbling for words, "I don't know if this is right to ask you."

"What is it, Sam?"

"I don't want to hurt your feelings, but I have a question."

"Sure, go ahead."

"How old will I be when you die?"

As soon as he said that, I knew this was a real conversation that had to happen. Whether or not he had any of the details of my condition, he was picking up on my fragility. He felt it in his pores. He was thinking about the pending loss of his pop.

"I don't know, Sam," I said. "I hope you'll be much older. But tell me what you're worried about."

Still without looking at me, he said, "I'll miss my pop."

"Sam," I said, "what do you think happens when I die?"

He thought about that a minute, then looked up. "You'll go to heaven."

"Okay. Do you think I'll be happy there?"

"Yes."

"Do you think I will still love you?"

"Yes."

"Will you still love me in the same way or in a different way?"

After a thoughtful pause, "The same."

"So you know you'll love me and I'll love you, just the same as we do now." There was a quiet moment, and then I asked, "Do you think you'll feel my love for you?"

"Yes," he said, "I think I will."

His shoulders, finally, relaxed. He looked relieved. I waited a moment, watching this sweet child try to fathom what all of this meant, praying that I was implanting thoughts in his heart and head that he would be able to access after my death. But then after a few moments I thought of one other thing that might be important for Sam to consider.

"And Sam," I added, "there's one more thing. If I'm in heaven, and I look at you and I see that you've started to lose your hair, I'll be laughing my butt off."

"No!" he yelled. "No! No! No!"

So Sam got the joke. And the message. Death does not interfere with love.

And I have the satisfaction of knowing there will come a day after I'm gone when he will look in the mirror, see himself starting to go bald, and hear me laughing my ass off. And feel all my love.

◈

After I talked to Sam, I thought about how much I love the people who have died—my parents, my sister, and my former wife, Sandy. Death has not diminished that. I once spoke with a Buddhist teacher who told me about the death of his brother several years earlier. He said, "I used to love my brother in a hundred different ways. And now I love him in 99 ways."

We associate death with sadness and longing, which is very natural. But the pain associated with death comes from the longing for something we had yesterday. Underneath the longing and the desperation is love. It's just that simple. If we didn't love, we wouldn't hurt. And the more we grasp, the more we suffer. So I stopped grasping even for my own life, and my heart opened more and I found myself able to love more easily. I even changed my relationship with my body. Instead of feeling resentment for what it was doing, I came to feel a deep gratitude for how hard it has been working to keep me alive for all these years.

I thought about the answer I had given to my professor in grad school who asked, "Do you exist?" Today, my answer would be different. Not "Who wants to know?" but "I do if I love." If I love, I know I exist. And the more I love, the more love I feel.

EPILOGUE

The Care Package

Dear Debbie and Pat,

So you've now experienced what it's like to raise a child from the age of zero to eight-and-a-little-more. One of the joys, for me, in writing this book has been the opportunity to recall so much that has happened with Sam. Being a grandfather has taken me into unexplored territory, and as I hope you can glean, it has been a wonderful journey, and I hope it continues for a long time. I knew my heart would be open to this child, but how could I anticipate the many ways he would help open it wider and wider—almost to bursting. I knew I would feel the same love that I felt for my own children. But I had no way of understanding, before it happened, how my love for him would magnify my love for you, for Ali, for my friends and neighbors and clients and colleagues and—sometimes, I think—for every creature on the earth and for the earth itself.

⛬⛬

We have talked over the years (and throughout the writing of this book) about raising the child you have rather than the child you want. Of course this is not always easy for parents who want to protect their child from adversity. A naturalist once said that in nature there are no rights and wrongs, only decisions and consequences. So if we work very hard to protect our children from distress, what are the consequences? We often behave that way because of our anxiety, so in the short run, we will have less anxiety. In the short run.

And what happens to our children if they are protected? Plenty. If we work too hard to clear away all adversity in their path, we steal something from them. We are learning that overprotected children are more self-absorbed, less resilient, and less creative. Anxiety disorders among our children are increasing. And much of this is because of anxious parents trying to protect their children. So how can we learn to tolerate our anxiety and have faith in our children's ability to tolerate some adversity?

It begins in infancy when we say "no" to our children and they cry. That's when we learn to tolerate our own discomfort in the service of good parenting. When they get older, setting limits becomes more important than ever. But parents should not become autocrats, doors should be open for discussion, and everyone's feelings should be listened to with respect before a decision is made.

When our children get older and have a conflict, we should listen to them rather than tell them what to do. If we do truly listen, we can give them gentle feedback about their ideas. And then we can send them back to try to resolve their conflict, whether it is with peers or teachers.

Of course, they won't always resolve their problems in a way that feels good. But typically we learn more from losing than winning. When children suffer adversity in school, failure on tests, or difficulty in relationships, this is an opportunity for them to develop their coping skills, to figure out that they can tolerate loss. This builds resilience.

So what happens when they leave home? Well, the parental touch must get even lighter. When they were small children and they ran into the street, we could pull them back. But now, when we see them walk into what looks like a risky situation, all we can do is offer advice and then hope that they change their minds.

∽⌾∾

When your sister, Ali, first got out of college, she was living with her boyfriend and working as a veterinary nurse in North Jersey. She was very unhappy—angry with the people she worked with and angry at the world. Since I knew this kid pretty well, I suspected she was depressed. I was also aware of how much anxiety I felt about her possible depression. Everything in me wanted to do something right away. My body and mind were saying it was an emergency.

But it really wasn't. Ali had been depressed and irritable off and on much of her life and I knew she was not suicidal. So despite the fact that it felt like an emergency and my impulse was to "insist" she do something right away, I knew some of the urgency came from my own distress. So I waited and just felt what I felt for a few days. As a result, it began to seem like less of an emergency. And I was also able to get a clearer picture of Ali. I knew that she could navigate the waters of adversity because I had seen her do it over and over.

So when I was able to get in touch with my own feelings, I experienced my great love for Ali. And then I knew what to do. I asked her if I could spend the day with her. She agreed. We walked her dogs, shopped for jeans, and just hung out at her house talking about her ideas for an outdoor enclosure for the dogs. But while we were hanging out, she was telling me about her life. And at the end of the day, I told her I understood how much she was suffering.

We sat quietly for a few minutes before I asked her if she would like to hear my thoughts about what was happening. When she said yes, I told her I thought she was depressed. I described what depression was and what it felt like for me when I was depressed.

She looked at me with those same sad, innocent eyes I saw when she was a child and said, "Dad, I thought everybody felt this way."

When I left Ali, I told her that I would be happy to help her pursue treatment. She never accepted my invitation, but she found treatment on her own and, after all these years, is still doing very well.

∽ᐧᐧᐤᐧᐧ∾

I have treated many parents of adult children who behave toward their children the same way they did when the kids were small. When there is a problem or a crisis in their lives, they jump in and do whatever they can to fix it, which inevitably makes things worse. Many of these parents come to me in their 60s and 70s, worried about their children in their mid-30s who seem to have no creative coping skills and still depend on their parents for money.

Every year we raise our children, we must release our grasp a little more. If we delay this process or postpone it, it gets worse for the whole family. The last thing any adult wants is to have her problems managed by her parents.

Several people in the meditation community have written books and articles about mindful parenting. This means being mindful about our own emotions toward our children at any given moment and not reacting to these emotions. Then we can be mindful about our children's emotions. After that, we are able to have a thoughtful, reflective response rather than a reactive one. And I think that is a great approach to parenting.

∽∂∾

One thing I don't worry about with Sam is what will happen if, or when, he decides to become a parent. The reason I don't worry is because he will have learned from you both.

But there is one stage that you have yet to experience, and I'm hoping I can help you and Ali and Sam with that. As I age, if I live more than another decade, I know I am at risk for increased forgetfulness and confusion. I hope you will treat me with love and compassion.

What am I saying? I know you will.

But here's the part that may be the most difficult for you.

As my own parents aged, my mother's health began to fail. She became confused and unstable. My father insisted on being her caretaker. He helped her dress in clothes that I knew she never would have worn, and they were often dirty. My mother cared a great deal about how she looked, and this was hard for me to watch.

When I asked him my father how he was holding up, he would always say, "Fine!" But I knew he wasn't.

My visits to their apartment were depressing. She would sit in one room and watch television, and my father would sit in the other, reading, almost as though they were just waiting for their lives to end.

One day before driving to Atlantic City to visit them, I was sitting on my back deck reading the paper when I heard a thunderous crack. I looked up and saw that a tall tree had fallen over and was leaning on another one that was strong and still very much alive. I remember thinking to myself, *I wonder if the strong tree knows the other one is already dead. I wonder if the strong tree knows that by holding that weak tree, its own health and stability are jeopardized.* And then there was another thunderous crack, and the living tree gave way, toppled by the weight of the tree it was supporting.

Then I realized that what I'd *thought* was the right thing to do with my parents might not be the right thing. I'd thought I should intervene and get help for both of them so they could stay together in their apartment. But the answer wasn't quite so black and white.

The next time I visited, instead of inviting my father to give me his pat answer, I told him about my confusion and how sad I felt about what was happening to both of them. He said he was sad also, then we both cried.

Several weeks later, my father asked me for some ideas about how he could get some help. (I have no idea whether his request was related to our discussion, but perhaps.) I found a geriatric social worker who came to the apartment, developed a relationship with both of my parents, and helped figure out what they needed to improve the quality of their daily lives. His presence was a great relief to all of us.

Several months later, we found out my mother's confusion was because of something called "normal hydrocephalus," an excess of water causing pressure on the brain.

We took her to a neurosurgeon at Jefferson Hospital who said he could help relieve the pressure by putting a shunt in the brain and draining some of the fluid. Because of her confusion, my mother thought it was brain surgery. My sister had died a couple of years earlier from a brain tumor and during that process she had had surgery several times. So my mother, in her confusion, thought she had something similar to my sister and refused the surgery.

Both the doctor and my father looked to me. I was clear about what we needed to do. Despite the fact that it would shorten her life and despite the fact that her judgment was impaired by her confusion, I wanted to respect her wishes and her dignity. The alternative was unthinkable.

My mother died several months later.

— Dad

Dear Sam,

I referred earlier to a Talmudic story I told you about how, before a child is born, God infuses that child with all of the wisdom he needs in life. But I have just discovered there is a follow-up to the story. Right before the child is born, an angel comes and slaps the baby on the face, causing it to forget everything that it's learned!

So why would this happen? First we learn, then we forget. Some rabbinic interpretations of this event have suggested that our task in life is to relearn what we once knew. I think that's true. People pay me lots of compliments about my speeches and books. They use words like "wise" and "insightful." But then I ask them if I said anything they didn't already know. Almost inevitably there is a moment of silence as they realize they have always known what I had to say, but had simply forgotten. Then I hear things like, "I guess I just needed to hear it again." So the rabbis were right.

But every now and then there is an uncommon child like you, Sam. You make me wonder if the angel got distracted and forgot to slap you before you were born. Right now, you seem to have more wisdom than most boys of your age. There is something inside of you that seems quiet and thoughtful, despite the fact that we all live in a world that feels noisy and sometimes thoughtless.

And because you have an uncommon brain, heart, and soul, you become a teacher—the one we all need to remind us of what is good and pure and true. You remind us of what we once knew.

You are uncommon, you are a teacher, you are a blessing, you are love.

— Pop

ACKNOWLEDGMENTS

I first met Patty Gift five years ago when she was my editor for *Letters to Sam*. At first, I loved the way she thought about the book. As I got to know her, I loved the way her mind worked. And then I grew to love the way her heart worked until, beautifully, they all worked together. She has been a wonderful guide and mentor, but how fortunate I am to call her friend.

One of the many gifts she gave me was my introduction to Reid Tracy, the CEO and president of Hay House. At our first meeting, Reid told me that Hay House was only about helping people and that every author they published had that as their goal. I remember thinking that this is a man who is leading an organization with both his mind and his heart. And then I noticed that for lunch he had eaten a half of a cheeseburger and half an order of French fries. And then I knew that he could balance matters of the heart with matters of the mind!

Among the wonderful people at Hay House who helped with the *Wisdom of Sam*, I thank Patty's assistant editor Sally Mason, copy editor Anne Barthel, and designer Bryn Starr Best.

I always acknowledge my agent, my friend, my counsel Edward Claflin, and I always will. We first met when he was my co-author with my first book, *Voices in the Family*. That was nearly 20 years ago, and not a week goes by that we don't talk on the phone or exchange e-mails. None of my books would have been published without his talent and his friendship.

Of course the real credit for this book goes to Sam. His sweetness could be felt well before he had words. But once he began speaking, his simple and honest observations about life showed us a child who wasn't just sweet but also insightful and compassionate and wise. So I thank Sam, my grandson, the love of my life, my pal, and a very unique child.

ABOUT THE AUTHOR

Psychologist **Daniel Gottlieb** is the author of *Letters to Sam* and *Learning from the Heart*, which have been published in 15 languages and received worldwide attention. In 2009, in the U.S., he was the recipient of the Books for a Better Life Award in the Motivational Book category for *Learning from the Heart*. The same year, in Taiwan, he received The Fervent Love of Life Award in recognition of the Chinese-translation version of *Letters to Sam*.

Gottlieb is also the author of *Family Matters*, recently reprinted as a trade paperback, and *Voices of Conflict; Voices of Healing*, a publication of People with Disabilities Press. He hosts an award-winning mental health call-in program, *Voices in the Family* and writes a weekly blog on the website of The Christopher and Dana Reeve Foundation.

A practicing family therapist as well as author and talk-show host, Gottlieb lives in Cherry Hill, New Jersey, where he has a private practice in individual and family psychotherapy. In 1979, when he was 23, Gottlieb had a car accident that rendered him quadriplegic. One year after the accident, he resumed his practice. He later served on the advisory board at Wordsworth Academy and The Boys & Girls Club of Camden, and from 1996 to 2000, he was on the National Advisory Council at the Center for Mental Health Services.

Gottlieb's radio program, *Voices in the Family,* can be heard weekly on the public radio station WHYY-FM 90.9 FM in Philadelphia. He is the recipient of numerous awards for the show, including a national Clarion Award, a Best Local Radio Program Award from the Society of Professional Journalists, a National Mental Health Media Award, and the Philadelphia Society of Clinical Journalists Lifetime Achievement Award. Other honors include the Excellence in Media Award from the Association of Marital and Family Therapy and the Pennsylvania Public Broadcasting Award.

NOTES

NOTES

NOTES

NOTES

NOTES

NOTES

NOTES

NOTES

NOTES

NOTES

NOTES

Hay House Titles of Related Interest

YOU CAN HEAL YOUR LIFE, the movie,
starring Louise L. Hay & Friends
(available as a 1-DVD program and an expanded 2-DVD set)
Watch the trailer at: **www.LouiseHayMovie.com**

THE SHIFT, the movie,
starring Dr. Wayne W. Dyer
(available as a 1-DVD program and an expanded 2-DVD set)
Watch the trailer at: **www.DyerMovie.com**

❧ ❧

BE HAPPY: Release the Power of Happiness in YOU,
by Robert Holden, Ph.D.

*EXCUSES BEGONE!: How to Change Lifelong,
Self-Defeating Thinking Habits,* by Dr. Wayne W. Dyer

*IT'S NOT THE END OF THE WORLD: Developing
Resilience in Times of Change,* by Joan Borysenko, Ph.D.

*I THINK, I AM: Teaching Kids the Power of
Affirmations,* by Louise L. Hay

❧ ❧

All of the above are available at your local bookstore,
or may be ordered by contacting Hay House (see next page).

We hope you enjoyed this Hay House book.
If you'd like to receive our online catalog featuring
additional information on Hay House books and products,
or if you'd like to find out more about the
Hay Foundation, please contact:

Hay House, Inc.
P.O. Box 5100
Carlsbad, CA 92018-5100

(760) 431-7695 or (800) 654-5126
(760) 431-6948 (fax) or (800) 650-5115 (fax)
www.hayhouse.com® • www.hayfoundation.org

ॐ

Published and distributed in Australia by: Hay House Australia Pty.
Ltd., 18/36 Ralph St., Alexandria NSW 2015 • *Phone:* 612-9669-4299 •
Fax: 612-9669-4144 • www.hayhouse.com.au

Published and distributed in the United Kingdom by: Hay House
UK, Ltd., 292B Kensal Rd., London W10 5BE • *Phone:* 44-20-8962-
1230 • *Fax:* 44-20-8962-1239 • www.hayhouse.co.uk

Published and distributed in the Republic of South Africa by:
Hay House SA (Pty), Ltd., P.O. Box 990, Witkoppen 2068 • *Phone/Fax:*
27-11-467-8904 • info@hayhouse.co.za • www.hayhouse.co.za

Published in India by: Hay House Publishers India, Muskaan
Complex, Plot No. 3, B-2, Vasant Kunj, New Delhi 110 070 • Phone:
91-11-4176-1620 • *Fax:* 91-11-4176-1630 • www.hayhouse.co.in

Distributed in Canada by: Raincoast, 9050 Shaughnessy St.,
Vancouver, B.C. V6P 6E5 • *Phone:* (604) 323-7100 •
Fax: (604) 323-2600 • www.raincoast.com

ॐ

Take Your Soul on a Vacation

Visit **www.HealYourLife.com**® to regroup, recharge, and
reconnect with your own magnificence.Featuring blogs, mind-body-
spirit news, and life-changing wisdom from Louise Hay and friends.

Visit **www.HealYourLife.com** today!